REMARKABLE

The Diversely United, Blood-Bought Church of Jesus Christ

CHRISTOPHER N. BEARD

Peoples Church Cincinnati

Produced with the assistance of the Barton-Veerman Company. Project staff include Dave Veerman, Bruce Barton, Ashley Taylor, Linda Taylor, Larry Taylor, Rose Tussing.

Scripture quotations taken from THE HOLY BIBLE, NEW INTERNATIONAL VERSION®, NIV® Copyright © 1973, 1978, 1984, 2011 by Biblica, Inc.™ Used by permission. All rights reserved worldwide.

Scripture quotations marked NASB taken from the NEW AMERICAN STANDARD BIBLE ®, Copyright © 1960, 1962, 1963, 1968, 1971, 1972, 1973, 1975, 1977, 1995 by The Lockman Foundation. Used by permission.

Scripture marked (KJV) is from the King James Version.

TABLE OF CONTENTS

Prologue   7

Introduction   9

Part I: Scriptural Underpinnings   11

    Chapter 1: The Church at Ephesus Was Remarkable   13

    Chapter 2: Why Ephesus Stood Out for Paul   15

    Chapter 3: Back to the Beginning   23

    Chapter 4: Back to Ephesus   25

Part II: Case Study—Stories from Peoples Church Cincinnati   29

    Chapter 5: The Beginning   31

    Chapter 6: First Steps   35

    Chapter 7: Race Mentors   39

    Chapter 8: Diverse Lay Leadership   41

    Chapter 9: Casting a Clear Vision   45

    Chapter 10: Pivot Point   49

    Chapter 11: Nations Inclusion   53

    Chapter 12: The Next Generation   57

    Chapter 13: Turning the Corner   61

    Chapter 14: The Gospel of Jesus Christ, Missions, and Biblical Justice   63

    Chapter 15: Awakenings   67

    Chapter 16: Full Circle   69

    Chapter 17: Orphans   71

    Chapter 18: Collective Impact   73

    Chapter 19: Crossonomics   75

    Chapter 20: We Were Not Alone   77

    Chapter 21: First Love   79

    Chapter 22: The Name Change   83

    Chapter 23: Christ Covets National Stage   85

    Chapter 24: Convergence   89

    Chapter 25: The *Los Angeles Times*, 100 Years after Azusa   91

Part III: Impacting Beyond   93

    Chapter 26: Ground Zero, Israel, and the West Bank   95

    Chapter 27: St. Louis (Ferguson)   97

Chapter 28: Global Church Implications
(One United Inclusive and Indigenous Church) 101
Chapter 29: Eleventh-hour Harvesters 103
Chapter 30: Change of Plans 107
Chapter 31: Racially Reconciling, Ethnically Inclusive, Diversely United 111
Chapter 32: Irrational Racial Fear 113
Chapter 33: 2014 117
Chapter 34: Tanzania 121
Chapter 35: Black Lives Do Matter 125
Chapter 36: Racially Reconciling Churches and American Cities 127
Chapter 37: University of Cincinnati, Peoples Church,
and Corinthian Baptist Church 131
Chapter 38: The Hard Work of Racial Reconciliation
Includes Racial Justice 135
Chapter 39: David Singleton 141
Chapter 40: The Work of the Church of Cincinnati 143

Part IV: Covenant Groups, Race to Unity, City Servants 145
Chapter 41: The Whole Church, the Whole Gospel, the Whole City 147
Chapter 42: Racial Myths Shattered 151
Chapter 43: Race to Unity 153
Chapter 44: Dismantling Idolatry in the Church 155
Chapter 45: City Servants 157
Chapter 46: MLB and Racial Justice Summit 161
Chapter 47: NPR 163
Chapter 48: Ta Nehisi Coates 165
Chapter 49: Dr. Mark Fairchild 167

Part V: Praxis 169

Praxis—Personal Life
Chapter 50: Diversifying Our Own Lives 173
Chapter 51: Music and Movies 177
Chapter 52: Friends 179
Chapter 53: Reflection 181

Praxis—Local Church
Chapter 54: Basics for Leading a Local Church into a Diverse Unity 187

Praxis—Church Collective
Chapter 55: Local Impact 217
Chapter 56: National Impact 229
Chapter 57: Global Impact 239

| TABLE OF CONTENTS |

Part VI: Endgame—Back to Theology · · · · · · · · · · · · · · · · 243

Part VII: Challenges and Hindrances · · · · · · · · · · · · · · · 255

Part VIII: Solutions and Tools · · · · · · · · · · · · · · · · · · · 263

Epilogue · 267

Addendums · 279
   Diagnostic Questions · 279
   Glossary of Terms · 281
   Resource List · 285

PROLOGUE

In 1995, a stirring began in my heart to experience something I had never seen before: a racially reconciling church, a church-like-heaven-on-earth, a local, nations-inclusive congregation of Jesus Christ followers (as described in Revelation 7:9) in my own city of Cincinnati, Ohio.

At the time, I was serving as an associate pastor in a midsize, historic Assemblies of God church located city center. Like most of the American church at the time, and even still today, we were a segregated homogenous church; but in our case, we were also a congregation of middle-class suburban commuters worshiping in the heart of a midsize metropolitan American city.

Not only did we worship mono-ethnically in the midst of a diverse population, we were also geographically positioned two miles from the former Mason-Dixon line, the Ohio River—the literal Civil War border between North and South. It was as if we were congregationally straddling the racial divide of America with almost exclusively white attenders from both Ohio and Kentucky, unaware of the irony and the impotence of our homogeneity in the face of historical irreconciliation.

What now was beginning to grow in my heart, seeded by the Holy Spirit, was the insight that as the church began to heal at the deepest fracture in American society—the black-white fissure—and to walk in diverse unity, such a demonstrated reconciling gospel of Christ would profoundly lead toward healing and health in our injuriously racialized society.

Further, I thought that as our own congregation put racial inclusion front and center, we would also invariably bloom with diverse ethnic inclusion. In other words, if intentional black/white reconciliation was a core heartbeat for us, we would see people from other nations and ethnicities coming to Christ and into the body as they witnessed seemingly unsolvable racial separation and its implications being forthrightly and faithfully addressed. And perhaps, through His reconciling gospel, a body of believers uniting in biblical evangelicalism and loving influence might consequentially bless our region.

"Let your light [so] shine before others, that they may see your good deeds and glorify your Father in heaven" (Matthew 5:16) was ringing in our hearts.

And, my goodness, did our city need substantive good works and to experience life-impacting, societal healing!

Within just a few years from these 1995 heart-stirrings from the Lord, our city was burning. In April 2001, a teenaged black man, unarmed and afraid, was shot and killed by police at the end of a chase initially triggered by arrest warrants for unpaid parking tickets. Cincinnati's civil unrest lit up national news. City authorities declared martial law and enforced a four-night 6:00 p.m. curfew. It was a warm spring break week between Palm and Easter Sundays, and the city was on fire.

Little had we understood how timely and relevant a gospel-centered, reconciling church and vision would prove to be. We never imagined twenty years ago how consequential this vision would still be at the time of this writing in 2019. The United States devolves further into racial and political discord, fractiousness, separation, and pain, and the church is seemingly frozen like a deer in headlights—unsure what to do, paralyzed, and off mission.

C. N. Beard
Jackson, Wyoming, October, 2019

INTRODUCTION

I welcome you to these pages. They are prayerfully written. The goal is to lay down a theology, a story, and practical learnings. I also want to provide resources to help you as a church leader follow what God is placing in your heart about planting, leading (or helping to plant or lead) a reconciling, diversely united church of the Messiah. Like me, you want your church to live out a robust gospel, one that reconciles people to the Father and to each other through Jesus Christ, and then to have a local and global impact.

In this book I will share how God moved Peoples Church Cincinnati from 98 percent white in 1995 to 30 percent African American, 30 percent international, and 40 percent Caucasian, both in our congregation and in our leadership structure.

I will share both story and praxis.

But first I want to lay down a theology from Scripture.

Without an undergirding scriptural theology, any effort to move a homogenous church toward a diverse future is susceptible to being a gospel-less effort in multiculturalism, political correctness, or trend-following. Unanchored in biblical principles—the "why"—you will break on the beach when the storms thrash your ship. And storms will thrash.

To underscore this thought, without rooting your effort in the why and leading both yourself and your congregation in a clear scriptural understanding of the church Jesus paid for, the enemy will destroy you. This work is not for the faint of heart, weak of mind, or prayerless.

And hear this: Not only is this vision full-gospel, I also believe Scriptures show it is requisite to God's strategic plan in the earth until the day of Christ's appearing for those who are His.

This study of God's plan *for* His church and *through* His church, and His endgame plan to bring all things under the authority of the Son (1 Corinthians 15:24-28), requires the reader to keep a copy of the Scriptures in hand. We will mention many verses, and I believe that prayerful Scripture reflection must underpin all that the Lord has in mind for and through your life in light of this vision: *A diversely united biblical church best embodies heaven's presence, will, and wisdom on earth and is itself God's strategic plan toward the endgame for all things* (see Matthew 24:14).

PART I

Scriptural Underpinnings

Chapter 1

THE CHURCH AT EPHESUS WAS REMARKABLE

From Acts 20, we know that the church at Ephesus was remarkable.

Paul was traveling one last time to Jerusalem. His missionary work was complete. God had something new in store for him now. He would be arrested, and his church-planting days would be over.

Acts 20 tells a special story. Traveling toward Jerusalem for Pentecost, Paul directed the ship to pull in at Miletus of Asia Minor, present-day western Turkey. Mind you, this was not like pulling your car off a twenty-first-century expressway. Paul and his team employed extraordinary effort to call a meeting of the local church leaders to share final thoughts for the Kingdom enterprise. There, thirty miles south of Ephesus, the apostle sent for the Ephesian elders.

In the port city meeting at Miletus, Paul provided crucial clues as to how special Ephesus was to him—insights Luke captured in writing for all of us, for all time.

» Paul had given the church at Ephesus the *whole* counsel (or will or plan) of the Lord (Acts 20:27).

» He had taught at Ephesus for three years. Nowhere else had he done that (Acts 20:31).

» He had taught and admonished them night and day with *tears*, with intensity from his whole being (Acts 20:31).

» He emphasized something important: "Be shepherds of the *church of God*, which he *bought with his own blood*" (Acts 20:28b, italics mine). (We will unpack this "blood-purchase" idea more later when we look at Revelation 5:9-10.) In fact, Paul said, "Keep watch over yourselves and *all the flock* of which the Holy Spirit has made you overseers" (Acts 20:28a, italics mine).

» Finally, Paul warned that "wolves" would try to divide the body there. These truth-distorters would not spare the flock! Paul feared division would come to the church at Ephesus. He charged the elders to defend their diverse unity (as the book of Ephesians will bear out). Their ability to hold together would be severely tested. Paul had arranged this unique meeting on the Miletus beach to punctuate that point.

When Paul finished speaking, he knelt down with them on the Aegean seacoast and prayed.

Then, at the beginning of the very next chapter, Luke emphasizes how Paul and his traveling team had to tear themselves away from the Ephesian elders (Acts 21:1).

Why?

Nowhere else in the New Testament do we see such intense language about Paul's departing from loved ones as we do here.

Perhaps, more than anywhere else, that church at Ephesus reflected the pinnacle expression of Paul's ministry calling, theology, mission, and vision? For certain, the Ephesian church was special. The question is, what made it so remarkable?

Chapter 2

WHY EPHESUS STOOD OUT FOR PAUL

Thank God for the epistle to the Ephesians. In it we see a likely summary and clear view into the content of Paul's only three-year, one-location teaching ministry. In light of him saying that he had given them the whole counsel of God (Acts 20:28), what he includes in the Ephesian letter is worth careful study.

To get a clear sense of what Paul is doing in this letter, I suggest reading the whole epistle through in one sitting, then join me in a closer study, beginning in chapter 2.

Ephesians 2 opens with salvation. We are now about to address the question of why the Ephesian elders merited Paul's last church leadership meeting.

You were dead in your sins. But because of His great love and mercy for us, God has made us alive with Christ, even when we were dead in sin! It is by grace we have been saved, through faith! (See Ephesians 2:1-9.)

As evangelicals, gospel-centered believers, we like to stop reading there and, thus, miss the progression of Paul's thought entirely. Where he goes next is astounding.

Ephesians 2:10 reveals that we are created in Christ Jesus "to do good works"! Societally impactful good works. Others-affirming good works. Good works of the Kingdom of God. Good works among and for believers and unbelievers alike.

As Bible-rooted evangelicals, we're often so careful about avoiding a works-based gospel that we inadvertently miss considering the sovereignly preplanned impact the Lord intends *through our redeemed lives.* Ephesians 2:10 is mind-blowing in that regard! That verse alone deserves ample thought, prayer, and reflection and is part of why Paul's teaching at Ephesus was remarkable. He was just getting started with mind-expanding thoughts. Immediately after 2:10, he paints a vision for the local church that I had missed my whole Christian life until recent years.

In Ephesians 2:11–3:6, Paul expresses God's concept of His church, including the local church (or else why did he write it to and for a local church at Ephesus?). Local church application is critical for every Christ follower reading this book.

So, what was Paul saying in Ephesians 2:11–3:6 that we may have missed?

1. Now in Christ, Jews and nations (*ethne*) are diversely united as *one* (2:14).
2. *Every barrier* (wall of hostility) is destroyed through the cross (2:16).
3. Both nations and Jews are *in one body* reconciled to God. (2:16).

Stopping with those three observations alone, we have some serious implications for today's church, especially since the church today is almost entirely siloed ethnically.

Remember the thought made famous by Martin Luther King Jr. decades ago? "The 11 o'clock hour on Sunday [in America] is the nation's most segregated hour" (referring to the time that most churches began their Sunday worship services.) Frighteningly, that is still true today in churches the world over (when you observe for diverse inclusion of proximal tribes, nations, languages, and peoples, and not just skin color alone).

With Ephesians 2:15—"His *purpose* was to create in himself one new humanity" (italics mine)—Paul elevated this *radical diverse unity,* in one organized entity, as the very *purpose of God.* This is consistent with the concept Luke uses in Acts 20:27 when quoting Paul speaking to these same Ephesian elders: "I have not hesitated to proclaim to you the *whole will of God*" (italics mine).

What does Paul say is the purpose of God through diverse unity? It is to create in Himself "one new humanity." One new humanity. One. One diversely united local congregation at Ephesus. By logical extension, if this is a purpose of His fulfilled at Ephesus, it also refers to diversely united congregations of Christians everywhere in all the earth. How could we say otherwise?

But why create in Himself one new humanity? What is the purpose of this? Just a few verses earlier, in Ephesians 2:10, we see the words, "created in Christ Jesus." There Paul explains, "For we are God's handiwork, *created in Christ Jesus* to do good works" (italics mine).

Allow me to pause and emphasize that the second person pronoun "you" is plural wherever it appears throughout this chapter, even from 2:1, where Paul says, "You were dead in your transgressions and sins." The significance of highlighting the plural "you" for every Western and Euro-trained reader is that we have nearly always individualized this passage. This is one key reason why we miss the meat of Paul's message about the multiethnic local church, the multiethnic church at large, and our understanding of the plan of God to raise up diversely united local congregations "created in Christ Jesus to do good works, which God prepared in advance" (2:10).

Did you catch all of that? Through the work of the Cross and the power of the Resurrection making alive all of us who were dead in our sins when we followed the ways of this world (including segregating ourselves from the "other"), we are now created into one new humanity, corporately in Christ Jesus, to do good works prepared in advance for us to do together!

That's the significance of the plurals "we" and "you" in this whole letter. What this does *not* mean is that we as individuals are off the hook, or that we are not individually precious to God or personally accountable. We are logically included in the plural as individual women and men created in His image who live in community with others.

But the plural pronouns are the key to grasping the richness of Paul's teaching here.

So now further into Ephesians 2 and 3, we will see that Paul adds even more nuance and insight to this revelational, revolutionary gospel that is uniting once-distant groups (and inherently, uniting diverse individuals, too) who once were apart from the Father and from one another. What are those insights?

» Through Christ Jesus, we all (Jews and nations) have access to the Father together (2:18).

» In Christ, we are all joined in one household, no longer strangers (2:19). We are multiethnic, multieconomic, diversely united.

» Joined together in the Lord, we rise as a holy temple (2:21).

» As a holy temple of diverse people, we are together a dwelling in which God lives by His Spirit (2:22).

In light of our racially and politically divided society today, which is as polarized as America has been in a long time, this church vision Paul painted holds huge significance for how the church does church. Ecclesiology (theology of church) matters!

As if to drive home the idea that this vision is for local churches, not just the church universal, Paul says to the Ephesians, "You too are being built together" (2:22).

So summarizing:
1. Dead in sins.
2. Alive in Christ.
3. A new creation together, diversely united in Him.
4. To do, as one, preordained good works.
5. A united body of redeemed diverse people, a household and a holy temple in which God lives, located in specific places all over the earth.

This is reformational, and the book of Ephesians has so much more still to teach!

Next, in Ephesians 3, Paul actually calls this diverse unity vision, this purpose of God through the Cross, his "insight into the *mystery of Christ*, which was not made known to people in other [prior] generations as it has now been revealed by the Spirit.... This *mystery* is that through the gospel the Gentiles [nations] are heirs together with Israel, members together of *one body*, and sharers together in the promise in Christ Jesus" (3:4b-6, italics mine).

The mystery of Christ. Not made known to generations before.

What did Paul just say it is?

He said it's that *through the gospel,* the nations are heirs *together* with Israel (the Jews) and *one body* in Christ Jesus.

But I thought that the mystery of Christ was the Cross itself, or personal salvation?

Well, for sure the work of the Cross has mystery, and the Cross is what makes the mystery of Christ possible. But the Cross is not the mystery to which Paul is referring here. Instead, the mystery now revealed is one diversely united body of Jesus—Jews and nations together.

This insight is so powerful to Paul's mind, and must be so threatening to darkness, that near the end of the Ephesian letter he writes, "Pray ... for me, that *whenever* I speak, words may be given me so that I will fearlessly make known the *mystery of the gospel*" (6:19, italics mine).

In Colossians 1, Paul calls this mystery:

... the word of God in its fullness—the mystery that has been kept hidden for ages and generations, but is now disclosed to the Lord's people. To them God has chosen to make known among the Gentiles the glorious riches of this mystery, which is Christ in *you* [plural, Jews and nations together] the hope of glory.

He is the one we proclaim, admonishing and teaching *everyone* [Jews and nations alike, on one body] with all wisdom, so that we may present *everyone* fully mature in Christ. To this end I strenuously contend with all the energy Christ so powerfully works in me." (1:25-29, italics mine).

Then Colossians 2:2-3 states, "My goal is that they may be encouraged in heart and [diversely] *united in love, so that they may have the full riches* of complete understanding in order that they may know the mystery of God, namely Christ, in whom are hidden *all the treasures* of wisdom and knowledge" (italics mine).

This is another surprise for me—namely, that a diverse body of Jesus united in love provides a more complete understanding of Christ Himself, of all the treasures of wisdom and knowledge that are in Him!

So back to the Epistle to the Ephesians, where we left off from Paul in chapter 3, explicitly defining the mystery of Christ as Jews and nations now united through Jesus and heirs together as one body.

Paul presses further into God's ecclesiological purposes. Ephesians 3:10–11 explains: "His intent was that now, through the church [the diversely united nations, *ekklesia*], the *manifold wisdom of God* should be made known . . . according to his eternal purpose that he accomplished in Christ Jesus our Lord" (italics mine).

This text has much we could discuss, but let's stay focused on this: The mystery of Christ, hidden for generations, is that through the gospel of Jesus Christ, Jews and nations are united as one body together. And so, through them together, the manifold wisdom of God is made known.

Through the cross, the church is united as one new body from Jews, nations, tribes, and tongues.

To combine some of the Ephesians 2 and 3 thoughts so far, Scripture says that through diversely united churches in which He dwells by His Spirit and through which good works take place, the kaleidoscopic wisdom of God is proclaimed. Again, incredible!

And to be even more exact, Paul actually says in 3:10b that the manifold wisdom is "made known to the rulers and authorities in the heavenly realms." Do we even begin to know what to do with this?

Now think of this. In this same book, from chapter 4 onward, Paul will explain to the Ephesians how the diversely united church is to function practically. He will also alert his readers in chapter 6 that hell itself will fight against this strategy, this plan, this mystery now revealed, and that the struggle is not against each other or people at all, but against forces of evil in the spiritual realm.

Okay, that's a lot of heavy sledding, thick reading. So let's take a breath. What are we seeing in Ephesians 2 and 3?

» We were dead in our sins.
» We are made alive in Jesus.
» We are made alive to be joined into a multi-ethnic, multicultural body.

» In this multiethnic, multilingual, multi-economic congregation produced through the gospel of Jesus Christ, people are reconciled to the
Father and to one another.

» Joined together, we are a temple in which He dwells.

» *That itself* is the mystery of Christ revealed, especially the uniting of
ethnic Jews and nations.

» Through this richly collected body of believers, good works He planned
in advance pour forth into society.

» Through this same diversely united church, God's rich wisdom is made
known.

» This not only impacts the earth but also the spiritual realm.

» And all of this is according to His eternal purpose that He accomplished
in Christ Jesus.

Knock me over. Crazy deep.

And now we begin to know what Paul meant in Acts 20:27 when he
said to the Ephesian elders at Miletus, "I gave you *the complete purpose* of
God. Now, defend it with all that is in you, take care of it. *Let no one divide
the flock*" (paraphrased).

Chapter 3

BACK TO THE BEGINNING

We have worked our way through a lot of information in Acts and Ephesians up to this point. Now let's look at some other passages. This is important because some will want to dismiss the work above as Pauline alone and not necessarily representative of the overall arc of Scripture, or even of the gospel. So let's consider this subject of the diversely united church from the Gospels and Genesis.

When Jesus gave the Great Commission, He planted a seed for the multi-peoples church. His words are not evasive or vague. "Make disciples of *all nations* [peoples, *ethne*]" (Matthew 28:19, italics mine). When the Lord said this, He was echoing content from the original Abrahamic covenant. In Genesis 12:1-3, God inaugurated His redemptive plan through calling a man, Abram, and explained: "*All peoples* on earth will be blessed through you" (italics mine).

As we see in the Great Commission of Matthew 28, the Lord was including this same vision.

In the moment of speaking the Great Commission to His Jewish disciples from a mountain in Galilee, Jesus could have been gazing across the Lake of Galilee toward the Decapolis (a Gentile region to the east of the sea) saying, "Go and make disciples of all nations."

From Genesis 12 to the end of Revelation, the plan of God has included a nations-full *ekklesia* (church) comprised of redeemed and reconciled Jews and Gentiles.

23

In fact, in John 17:20-23, at the last meal with His eleven disciples (those who remained after Judas left), Jesus asserted a link between profound unity among His *future* followers and the Great Commission's fulfillment. Jesus prayed, "Father unite them, not just these eleven, but those who will believe after them; unite them so profoundly that the world will believe that I am the Messiah (the One sent by the Father)" (my paraphrase).

Embedded in this prayer is the plutonium fuel for God's plan in all the earth for all eternity—a diversely united body under Christ that attracts and includes believers from all nations.

Jesus prayed *this* prayer over His nuclear team just hours before He went in obedience to the Cross. This prayer provides tremendous insight into the mind of God as to how His redemptive effort would thereafter unfold.

Naturally, the disciples didn't comprehend. Not for some time.

Chapter 4

BACK TO EPHESUS

We saw earlier how special Ephesus was in Luke and Paul's minds. But what we haven't yet mentioned is how central a role the Ephesian church plays in much of the New Testament.

In early 2016 I experienced my first sabbatical. As part of the planned seven-week reprieve for respite and study, my wife, Jan, and I traveled to western Turkey to visit friends. In preparation for our visit, our host asked if we'd be interested to see the archeological site of Ephesus since the flights there from Istanbul were easy and inexpensive. What a treat!

With just a tour guide and our friend, we spent half a day exploring this massive Roman-era archaeological site.

Near noon, as we were standing in front of the historic Celsus Library façade, our guide mentioned that after lunch we would see St. John's Basilica. Squinting at him in the sunlight, I inquired, "St. John's?"

The Turkish Muslim guide replied, "Yes, your apostle John!"

Then looking out toward the sea, I queried, "Where is Patmos?" Somehow in my years of undergrad, seminary, and sermon preparation studies, I had never closely looked at the geography of western Turkey, biblical Asia Minor.

He lifted his hand and pointed to the southwestward from where we stood on smoothed-over first-century stones. "Out that way, beyond what we can see."

After lunch, we visited John's traditional burial site with the famous baptismal (depicted on this book's cover).

My mind flooded with the immediate realization that John must have finished his ministry here, from Ephesus. Later I learned that likely his *last twenty years* were centered from this city, with *this* congregation as a home base—the same church into which Paul had poured three years of his ministry life; the same church where Paul had stationed his prize pupil, Timothy, to pastor in his absence; the same church addressed by Jesus first among the seven in John's Revelation.

Along with the other learnings yielded during sabbatical study from Acts 20 and the book of Ephesians, the implications for me were stunning. John was the disciple who lived the longest. By church tradition, he was the only one to die a natural death. As I researched later, John likely wrote his Gospel from Ephesus, his epistles, and the Revelation itself from that same spiritual, ecclesiological, and theological milieu.

Said another way, the church at Ephesus—with its rich, diverse, relational capital and theological depth, which we know from Paul's Ephesian epistle—provided the experiential and congregational "soil" from which John's writings sprang.

From that realization from the western Turkey experience came these observations (as we continue to consider scriptural underpinnings for church as heaven on earth and the role of the church at Ephesus as exhibit A):

» John is who includes in his Gospel what Jesus prayed at the Last Supper: "I pray for those who will believe in me . . . that all of them may be one . . . so that the world may believe that you have sent me" (John 17:20-23).

» John is who explains in his first epistle that salvation by necessity includes both belief in Jesus Christ and love of neighbor. First John 3:23 says, "How do you know you're in the truth? You believe in Jesus Christ *and* you love" (my paraphrase)

» John's Revelation includes again and again the refrain, "Every tribe, language, people and nation."

Also relevant to the role of Ephesus in the scriptural foundations of God's strategic plan is the fact that Paul wrote 1 Corinthians from there. This all the more shines a light on the essentiality of an interlocking, diversely gifted body (1 Corinthians 12). And he wrote his epistles to Timothy while the young man pastored the church there (1 Timothy 1:3). From the story in Acts, we know that Priscilla and Aquila taught there, as did Apollos (Acts 18:19, 24).

Christendom's center was at Ephesus for nearly four hundred years until moving north to Byzantium, today's Istanbul.

The significance is found in what Paul stated in Acts 20:27, "I have not hesitated to proclaim to you [Ephesian elders] the whole will of God."

PART II

CASE STUDY

Stories from Peoples Church Cincinnati

Chapter 5

THE BEGINNING

In early April 2001, Cincinnati was burning. Ezra Maize (the pastor of an historic black church), Joe Andino (a Spanish Pentecostal church planter), our kids' pastor Kevin Salkil, and I poured into Ezra's car and drove to an urban core located at Taft High School to hear from the police chief how clergy might help bring calm in this flashpoint moment. We felt like we might be a Spirit-led reconciliation crew, but we had no idea what we were going to see and hear and what, if any, part we might play.

As we prayerfully drove among the cordoned-off streets, we looked deeply into the eyes of the protesting young men longing for justice from the depths of their being. In recent years more than ten black men had lost their lives to police violence. Not one officer had yet been held accountable in any meaningful way. Each death was not of a complete innocent, but neither had they received the benefit of trial, judge, and jury.

In this current case, nineteen-year-old Timothy Thomas was unarmed, on foot, and on his way to buy a few things for himself, his girlfriend, and their newborn child. At the end of a foot chase, he was shot right in the chest. Based on Cincinnati's recent history between officers and young black men, he had had meaningful cause to fear and run.

Isaiah 59:4, 14-16 declares,

> No one calls for justice; no one pleads a case with integrity. They rely on empty arguments, they utter lies; they conceive trouble and give birth to evil. . . . So justice is driven back, and righteousness stands

31

at a distance; truth has stumbled in the streets, honesty cannot enter. Truth is nowhere to be found, and whoever shuns evil becomes a prey. The LORD looked and was displeased that there was no justice. He saw that there was no one, and he was appalled that there was no one to intervene.

Now four young pastors—two white, one black, and one Latino—were driving among the labyrinth of smoldering streets where hearts were on fire for some sense of justice.

Justice was not coming.

Amazingly, just four weeks earlier, the Lord had prompted our first step toward becoming a multiracial church staff. The March 4, 2001, *Cincinnati Enquirer* published a full-page story, "Divided by Race," with a score of civic leaders, black and white, dialoguing on how to heal our city racially. The group had no white clergy.

I brought that full-page piece to our staff meeting, laid it on the table, and expressed to the team how I believed we were to be a part of that discussion. My intention was to reach out to the newspaper editorial team and ask to be included at the table, that we had much to learn and wanted to be a part of the solution. One from our team looked around the circle at our all-white staff and stated the obvious. "Chris, what do we have to bring for that discussion? Look at us! What credibility do we offer?"

I knew he was right, but I also felt a call pulsing in my chest toward the work of a reconciler. I acknowledged the fact of our monochromatic reality as a church leadership team, but I also argued that we had already been clear to the board and body that we were going somewhere new in terms of racial inclusion. We were not going to look or be the same for much longer.

But commuting home that day, I cried out. "Lord, he's right! Why would the *Cincinnati Enquirer* accept me into this discussion? Help us, God. Help us diversify our leadership team. I don't even know where to begin."

The very next morning I received a phone call from my dear friend Ezra Maize. Our friendship had started some years before. His church met close by. Because they had no baptismal pool, a couple of Sundays each year he would bring twenty to thirty people for an afternoon baptism service, numbers which always blew me away.

We liked each other, laughed easily together, and prayed together for our Uptown Cincinnati neighborhoods and city. Some five years before, the Lord had prompted me to forge personal friendships with pastors of color, to love them, learn from them, live and serve in the Kingdom together, become like family. Novel idea. This had happened for Ezra and me.

Now, just hours after that commute home, Ezra was on the phone. "Chris, are you ready for your first assistant pastor of color?"

I was speechless. "Are you serious, or are you messing with me?" I asked. Perhaps one of our team had put him up to a practical joke with me; Ezra likes fun, and so does our staff.

But no. Ezra said, "Chris, I'm serious. I need a break from senior pastoring. Can I come join your team for a year before going back to church leading?"

I was stunned. My eyes filled with tears as I realized God was doing this: The Lord of the harvest, history, and hearts was answering my prayer: Ezra was calling me at the Spirit's prompting for such a time as this. Little did we know that one month later, our city would be experiencing violent racial grief and unrest and would be blanketed under martial law and a 6 p.m. curfew. God has timing.

Our April 2001 board meeting was held away from the church campus during that Cincinnati-proper curfew week. In that meeting, Ezra and his wife, Andrea, accepted an invitation from Jan and me and our board to join the church staff as the associate pastor.

On Easter Sunday, at the end of that martial law week, we announced to the church that Ezra and Anni were joining our team. The church erupted with relief and joy. Just four weeks before, Ezra had preached both morning services, and First Christian Assembly of God (our prior name) had fallen in love with this man and his family. The richness of his preaching, the example of his marriage and children, the charisma in his life from God's gifts in him, and the timing of the Lord in light of our city's crisis were clearly ordained from heaven.

First Christian Assembly would never be the same. And our city would be blessed by this local church transformation.

Chapter 6

FIRST STEPS

The way in which Pastor Ezra would join our team was important to me. He was leaving the pastorate of an important AME Zion church in our city. If people came with him, weakening that church, what good to the overall racial unity in the church of Cincinnati would that be? How Kingdom would that be? Not much.

So I asked him, "Please Ezra, would you ask people to stay at St. Mark and not come with you?" He agreed, except for two couples that he and Anni were personally discipling. These young marrieds had recently come to Christ and needed to stay connected. I pleaded, "Please Ezra, only those four." He agreed, and that's what happened.

Years later, these two couples would prove essential to what God was doing at Peoples Church Cincinnati.

When the new pastor for St. Mark came to follow Ezra there, we threw a welcome party as our locations were close. We let this new local church leader and his wife hear our heart and intentions. For all the years this pastor served in our city, our relationship was authentically one of mutual blessing. Their church flourished under his leadership.

With Ezra on our pastoral team, we learned so much. His preaching, leadership, insights, and honesty caused tremendous spiritual growth in us, as well as increasing racial awareness and cross-cultural growth in me and in our congregation.

One simple example of this took place at an AutoZone. Ezra and I had walked out of the church building together one day to go grab lunch.

A disheveled man walking across our parking lot asked us for twenty dollars to buy a small auto part. Ezra said, "Hop in with us!" We drove to AutoZone with the man in our back seat. Ezra's compassion was impactful. So was his wisdom.

At the store, we found the part was only a few dollars. After the purchase, I scooped the part off the counter and headed toward the exit. Ezra touched my arm to stop me and said, "Chris, get a bag."

The small part fit in the palm of my hand, so I replied, "I don't need one," and continued striding toward the door.

Again, Ezra stopped me and asked why I wasn't getting a bag.

"Ezra, we have the receipt and don't need a bag."

As we reached the sidewalk outside the store, Ezra paused one more time, and then asked me something I had never concerned myself with all my life, "You've never been stopped leaving a store, have you?"

Immediately I understood how different seemingly innocuous life moments can be for a man of color in comparison to my own life. This was an "aha" moment for me. Ezra explained, "If you were a black man, right now you'd be spread-eagled against that wall." It was the first time I viscerally experienced the two worlds Ezra and I lived in, one for the majority culture and another for everyone else, especially African Americans.

Racial fear, racism, racialization in our society was *real*. I knew so, because Ezra was my friend, and what had just occurred was spontaneous and without premeditation. It was a glimpse into his world as he experienced it daily. Because he was my friend, we could talk about race matters and weigh them together respectfully but also authentically, without inhibition or fragility. Many days of racial mentoring took place from Ezra's life to mine that year.

We returned to our passenger in the car and proceeded to his broken-down car just another few blocks away. He wanted to be dropped off short of the spot, but Ezra insisted he take us to the car. What happened next was so funny to me and yet sad at the same time. We pulled into the gas station and the car in question was actually up on blocks, no tires. Ezra handed him the small auto part and said, "Looks like you need a little more than this." The man quickly exited our vehicle before Ezra or I could offer prayer, embarrassed that his story was uncovered. Disregarding his lie, he was a life in need and a man who matters to God. Over the next years I would learn just how many obstacles were stacked against young men of color, probably some of the same factors debilitating this very man's life.

For many years I've reflected on the racial revelations I experienced that warm summer day outside of AutoZone.

Chapter 7

RACE MENTORS

After a year, true to his word, Ezra and Andrea went back to senior pastoring, eventually moving from Cincinnati altogether. Through the years we have had spontaneous and fun surprise reconnections, and our love for each other remains deep.

The two couples who came with them stayed and slowly began to rise in leadership within the church. More on that later.

But my intellectual and spiritual thirst to deepen and enrich my level of cross-racial understanding was increasing. If as a church we were going to be a factor, through Christ in us, toward healing the deepest divide in our city, in the nation, and in the church—the black/white fracture—we would have to prioritize this area of reconciliation. That meant my life needed to move from racially naive, insensitive, and ignorant to circumspect, honoring, and informed. My preaching and exposition of the Word would need to become more inclusive: my stories, my humor, my text selections, and my teaching series.

I had so much to learn.

I remember the Sunday I met Rose Sherman. In that early 2000s service, I noticed, from the platform, a tall, professional-appearing man of color. With still so few at that time, when I saw any African Americans in a service or in our café area, I did whatever necessary to meet and build a connection to them. After introducing myself to the tall man whose name was Ralph, the fashionably dressed elderly woman next to him said with an ornery twinkle in her eye, "Sure, introduce yourself to my nephew, but I'm actually one of your parishioners! I'm Rose Sherman. Nice to finally meet you, Pastor!" I was embarrassed and asked how long she'd been attending and whether we could meet over coffee. I wanted to hear this stately woman's story. She lit up at my request, and after an initial joy-filled, enriching visit, we began a monthly mentoring session. A mentoring of *me*.

I rarely saw her nephew Ralph again, but God had used him to connect me to Rose Sherman. For several years, Jan and I would visit Rose at her independent living facility every month. She was in her early eighties but was still a fiery, creative, funny, prayer-filled woman of God. In her day, she had been the first national officer of color for Girl Scouts of America. She had also spent many years of her life as an "organizer" in Oakland, California, during the Civil Rights movement. I had no idea what she meant by an "organizer" until many years later. Her father had owned a florist shop in Cincinnati, a matter of tremendous pride. At one time it was our city's longest-held African American–owned business. Life and years have now taught me what a big deal that was. After her brother's passing, the shop closed. Many in our city grieve that loss.

Never married, living single and retired back home in Cincinnati, Rose had heard the Lord speak to her heart to attend First Christian Assembly of God (our church's prior name). Even as I write this, I thank Him for sending her to us in those formative years. Rose prayed for Jan and me, coached us, shared her life stories, gave me reading assignments, laid hands on me for prayer again and again, and simply "discipled" this young pastor in what living black in America was really like, no matter how much you loved Jesus and had your life rooted in the gospel.

I profoundly appreciate those mentoring years and know they were essential to my formation as an emerging reconciler. Rose's prayers over me were passionate, expansive, and visionary, and went deep into my soul. I love and miss her dearly.

Life-friends, life-mentors of color—some who were in Christ and some who were not—have proven essential to the racial awareness and American history expansion I need my whole being marinating in for me to credibly lead the church into a more complete gospel-centered, racially reconciling future.

Chapter 8

DIVERSE LAY LEADERSHIP

Ezra's joining our staff was catalytic. He was an essential leader among us for our initial year of multiracial growth. But only one senior leader ethnically different to the majority does not equate to power sharing or unquestioned diverse inclusion. And authentically shared, diverse leadership authority is requisite for credible, racially reconciling church life.

Now even Ezra had moved on.

So we did whatever we could to demonstrate our unflinching commitment to become a church more reflective of Revelation 7:9 on earth, in Cincinnati.

Momentum from diverse inclusion catalyzed by Ezra's leadership among us propelled us forward.

Another early catalyst proved to be this: Our worship pastor, hired in 2002, was white but played the piano from his soul with rich gospel rhythms and sounds. He intentionally varied the worship selections to include minority and gospel and blended sounds, lyrics, and styles. People noticed. Some left; many came. We were experiencing multiracial, multicultural traction.

Another one: Our kids' pastor was white but married to an Hispanic woman. Together they were brilliant at welcoming children of all backgrounds and guiding our mostly white volunteer staff in how to create a culturally and ethnically inclusive ministry. Within a few years, our kids' volunteers and staff would become as diverse as the adults in the church.

By 2004, we had grown to about 5 percent African American and 5 percent international.

For Wednesday night church, we began intentionally inviting, including, and ministering to racially and economically diverse kids from our surrounding neighborhoods. Testimonies and stories from this new ministry shared at our weekend services stirred hearts and increased a gut-level love and commitment by the church for racial and economic inclusion we had never experienced before. And this was growing in our lay leaders and staff. I include "lay leaders" because by 2004 the pastors and I were no longer alone in fueling the vision.

Neighborhood families began attending on the weekends, and new diverse attenders from the suburbs were also joining as they saw the mix as so attractive and Kingdom-like.

This was an unexpected benefit. Even as our economic mix was diversifying downward from economically diverse growth, our finances felt the stabilizing of new arrivals of means attracted by the vision. Ex-offenders—white, brown, and black—sitting next to doctors and CEOs—white, brown, and black—became normal. One body, many parts. This aspect of New Testament Christianity was feeling so good to all of us, even as all of us, new and old attenders alike, were being culturally stretched.

Importantly, by 2004 we also had a diverse deacon board (the official board of the church). Getting there was not easy, and it didn't happen by "natural process" alone, which was simply not going to work as fast as we needed. So what did we do?

In prayer one day, we realized there was a natural choice for our board for our first person of color: Russell Johnson.

Russell had attended for twenty years or so. He had been part of our 2 percent diversity in 1995. He was a vocalist in the worship team, a godly brother, and a man loved and respected in the church. But after looking into it, I found he wasn't an official member. Nonmembers aren't board-eligible and we had a two-year minimum requirement before election eligibility.

We knew he was electable and didn't want to lose any more time. So I asked Mr. Johnson to lunch where I shared the vision on our hearts for a racially reconciling church. He was effervescent at the vision. I asked if he would help us by officially joining the church as a member and thereby become board-eligible after two years. He laughed gently and then allowed, "I'm really not a board type of person."

"Russell," I appealed, "without African Americans in decision-making leadership roles, how will we have any credibility in reconciling the body?"

He agreed to pray on it and soon officially joined the church. Sure enough, two years later he was nominated for the deacon board. Russell's life was so respected by the congregation.

But then he declined the nomination! Oh man. I asked for another lunch. There I pleaded with him. By now he had heard my heart in preaching and had observed the racial and ethnic growth within the body, but he was simply reticent to serve in that role. "Please, sir, please. Would you reconsider in light of the call of God growing within us to become a church-like-heaven-on-earth, every tribe and tongue?"

Thankfully, Russell accepted the nomination and was landslide-elected to the deacon board. Throughout the next years, God used Russell in so many profound ways to help guide the church forward. Soon, other men and women of color and non-Euro descent were being added to our board. We've never looked back with regard to balanced ethnic board inclusion. That is not to say that we don't stay carefully vigilant. We see our deacon board needing to be like the leadership team at Antioch: a diverse microcosm of the church like Jesus paid for on the Cross (Acts 13:1-2; Revelation 5:9-10).

Chapter 9

CASTING A CLEAR VISION

At my 2001 pastoral installation service, Bishop Michael Dantley—a leading pastor of color in our city and a heart-level personal friend and mentor—challenged me before the congregation from Habakkuk 2:2 to write down the vision and make it plain so the people could run with it.

Over the course of the next three years I prayed, listened, and retreated regularly to craft a new mission, vision, and core values for us to consider as a church, in light of all God had been stirring in me since early 1995 when I was twenty-seven.

In the spring of 2004, I shared and discussed the results with the staff, deacon board, and church body.

After key meetings and discussions with the staff and board to explore this content with them and receive their input, we used a seven-week sermon series plainly titled "Vision" and rolled out the results of that work from the pulpit and in writing.

God was calling us to become a racially reconciling, generationally rich, life-giving church thriving in the heart of the city. Along with personal righteousness, we would now also value societal righteousness. Along with evangelism and international missions, we would now equally honor biblical and racial justice work in our city and nation as essential to the full proclamation and demonstration of the gospel of Jesus Christ.

That same spring I was in much prayer about asking Brandon Wilkes to consider leaving his financially secure career with Procter & Gamble and join our pastoral staff as executive pastor. Jan and I had been prayerfully observing the lives and leadership of Brandon and his wife, Dorothy, since Ezra and Andrea's departure in 2002. The Wilkes were one of the two couples the Maizes had brought with them in 2001, and they had stayed when Ezra had returned to senior pastoring. Jan and I had invited Brandon and Dorothy soon after their arrival in 2001 to join the small group meeting in our home.

We so love this family. They quickly grew deep in the Lord, in the Word, and in their prayer life. Their marriage and parenting were healthy—qualities we look for in potential key leaders—and impressive for a couple so new in the Lord. We saw in them future pastors for our church.

And in early 2004 as I prepared to preach the "Vision" series, the Spirit prompted us to invite Brandon onto staff. Over lunch when I introduced the idea, Brandon chuckled disbelievingly at first, like, "You're kidding right?" But I wasn't.

I shared with him that I saw a calling on his life. That I believed he and I, together, could help lead our quickly diversifying body forward in Christ. I shared that I valued his wisdom, his sincerity in Christ, his family life, and his passion for people and for the Word of God. The church would pay for his seminary training (which he would later complete via extension from Trinity Evangelical Divinity School in Deerfield, Illinois). Would he pray about this?

Brandon agreed to pray. The sacrifice would be very real. The church could not compete with his P&G income. But . . . would he still pray? He would. He did. And with Dorothy's encouragement, Brandon stepped onto our pastoral staff on tax day, April 15, 2004. We laugh when we remember the date because to know Brandon is to know how much he hates paying taxes or spending *any* money for that matter! Not saying he's tight, just frugal.

Soon I heard pushback from some congregants about Brandon's hiring. "You hired him just because he's black." "It seems you like 'them' more than you like 'us.'"

These kinds of comments astounded me and, if I'm honest, offended me. They saddened me, too. Sometimes words like these made me so angry. But they were from hearts that were ensconced in "fleshy" ("carnal," we used to say), worldly worldviews (2 Corinthians 5:16 was helpful to us at these times). In some instances I mishandled conversations over these frustrating and misguided critiques. Instead of teaching in love, I would get defensive and argumentative.

Yes, Brandon was hired in part because he was black. He was also one of the most outstanding candidates I'd ever helped recruit for developing into the pastorate. The church had taken the same kind of risk on me and my predecessor, Clyde Miller. We were both in our early thirties when we were elected to actually *lead* this historic, multigenerational church. But we were given room to grow, mature, and develop.

We often did (and do) that very same thing with all our staff positions. We hire people with godly potential and mentor them into the incredible pastors He has created and called them to be. Brandon had the character, the gifts, the potential, and the calling.

His hiring was from the Lord.

The church shook—in both good and bad ways. Both because of the "Vision" sermon series and Brandon's hiring. People left. And people came. It was an electric spring. That summer was to be even more so.

Chapter 10

PIVOT POINT

Sunday, July 4, 2004—All the night before I had wrestled with the Lord about my sermon, and lost.

My "hip" was about to be dislodged, too.

I remember having prepared a message about reaching lost Americans, about how much the people of our country need Jesus. And they do.

But the Lord wanted something different. A lot different. He wanted a heart surgery on the church, and on me.

"Chris, I want you to address idolatry of America in the hearts of My Caucasian sons and daughters in the church."

I remember telling the Lord, "No way." So we wrestled. All night.

You may know what that's like. He gives you something to do that you just know will be painful. Painful to you, painful to others. Not bad pain, good pain, but pain nonetheless. Like surgery.

So on that July 4, in a still predominantly white church, though unmistakably in transition toward racial and ethnic inclusion, I emphasized heavenly citizenship as our primary identity as the people of the Kingdom. Of course, we have our earthly and national identities, but to the degree we over-spiritualize them or allow patriotism and nationalism into our hearts, to that same degree we're susceptible to idolatry.

And it was July 4.

Oh my.

The church was quiet. Very quiet.

We sang no patriotic songs. I talked gently about not overlaying the Cross with a flag, symbolically speaking. I talked about a new kind of nationalism, not as Americans but as the people of God, a holy nation, a chosen generation with a Kingdom intensity and a Christ identity, one that unifies all believers regardless of their background (Philippians 3:20; 1 Peter 2:9).

I taught how unchecked patriotism in believers' hearts—*believers' hearts*—divides the church and confuses us in our true identity in Christ Jesus. This is especially so in the white part of the American church where the flag affects so much idolatrous allure and for nearly everyone else carries so much sinful, hurtful baggage.

That day I submitted this for thought to the congregation: To the degree we celebrate July 4 as a big deal without equally celebrating July 2, the anniversary of the signing into law the Civil Rights Act of 1964 (it was the fortieth anniversary of that signing as I preached that day), to that same degree we separate ourselves black and white in the American church. That received a pretty quiet reaction, although a smattering of slow nods.

I shared stories from my friends of color who explained how uncomfortable they felt in church services where hands were raised to "God Bless America" as if it were a worship song to the Lord, and how offensive it was to hear the Founding Fathers of America enshrined as spiritual heroes to the church of Jesus. How were descendants of slaves to agree with that? And as one friend helped me to see, "How do we hope to rid the church of racism while at the same time upholding racist slave owners as Christian heroes?" Indeed.

The church shuffled out that day like after a sad funeral. And a kind of death it was.

I was heart-stricken. My "hip" hurt, too (like Jacob in the Old Testament). I knew I had been obedient to the Lord and to teaching what He had been showing me for some years, but I also saw friends and loved ones shaken to their core. Like me when I first started thinking about these things some years earlier, they would experience an identity free fall, a disorientation of sorts, a disillusionment until they landed on their Rock, their Savior, discovering their true identity is in Jesus Christ their King, not their earthly country.

That Sunday as I stepped off the platform after our second service, the Lord had an encouragement for me.

Nearly bounding down the aisle to greet me was a sharp couple of color I had never met before. This was their first Sunday, and they were exhilarated and so encouraging about the content of the message. As I listened to their story of job relocation from New Orleans, I rejoiced. As I rejoiced, I also heard in my spirit, "This couple will be the future youth pastors here."

Four years later Dele and Oneya Okuwobi came on staff for a nine-year run in leadership before moving on to pioneer their own Kingdom initiatives.

But on that day, that July 4 Sunday, they were sent by the Holy Spirit to help me understand this was just the beginning of an influx of new people—white, black, and brown—who would be captivated by a bigger vision than "Take America Back." They were yearning for the calling to be ambassadors together of another Kingdom, another government, one with a truly Christ-centered beginning and Christ-centered culture, so that all Americans and immigrants might be introduced to the King and His Kingdom.

Chapter 11

NATIONS INCLUSION

From the beginning of our church transition, we had a sense that if we unabashedly prioritized toward healing in the deepest divide in the American church—the black/white chasm—people from other nations would join, attracted by a spirit of humble, authentic inclusion. A caution in our spirits, and in large part a learned wariness gained through earnest discussions in cross-racial friendships, was that without a laser focus on racial reconciliation, we would become ethnically diverse, but we wouldn't be racially reconciling. That proved to be wisdom from the Lord and from our friends of color.

For fear of facing the fractious, painful issues of race, many multiethnic churches stay general in their vision and gain internationals or ethnic minorities but wonder why they are missing whites or blacks.

The Lord has helped us nourish this priority. We are grateful to have stayed effective regarding Kingdom matters of racial justice and reconciliation through intentional and laser-focused passion regarding black-white matters, but not to the exclusion of other significant cultural and ethnic conciliation and inclusion priorities.

The vision of church-like-heaven-on-earth requires making complex things simple and the ability to multitask authentically without loss of richness across a diverse spectrum of issues.

By 2004, we were experiencing profound enrichment from the diverse inclusion of many new African American congregants whom we celebrated for their personal perspectives, gifts, and uniqueness as well as for their cultural and collective contributions. Our church was changing for the better every day by their lives among us. That year was proving crucial and anointed in so many ways.

During that summer God was nurturing another pivotal relationship for us: the friendship between Petros Yefru and me.

By his presence and the East Africans he was co-leading, we were seeing fresh new proofs regarding the wisdom of prioritizing our church vision toward black-white American reconciliation. The East Africans saw spiritual fruit that was attractive to them. They also longed to experience welcome and inclusion by both white and black Americans. Neither was a given in their Monday-through-Saturday work and community experiences.

An important aside: This American social construction of black and white, this deepest fracture in the church in Cincinnati and the nation, is only the deepest because of the near complete genocide/ethnic cleansing of Native Americans from the American evangelical church, not to mention from America. Otherwise a Caucasian-Native American fissure might hold the position of the deepest church fracture needing reconciliation focus.

Now back to our 2004 story. Our church was about to experience a huge new surge forward as church-like-heaven-on-earth.

Petros and I had first met in 1997 when a pastor friend from another city had asked an Ethiopian ministry leader to drive to Cincinnati and introduce Petros to me. Petros, who had recently immigrated to Cincinnati with his Ethiopian wife, was discipling nine young believers from Eritrea and Ethiopia. He was looking for an American pastor who would love them, welcome them, baptize them, and include them as part of an American congregation.

Discerningly, Pete understood that if he baptized these recent converts, they would see him as their pastor and would want to form a separate ethnic/language church. A far-sighted man, Petros knew this would be a problem. So he made the case to his small group that the children they raised here would be Americans. He persuaded them to understand they had much to contribute in the American church, and conversely, much that they would receive.

Yet they also needed to have weekly fellowship in their own language where they could support one another culturally and practically as first-generation immigrants navigating this new American life. Pete would continue to lead a Sunday afternoon language fellowship for them, but in the mornings they would root themselves in a gospel-centered American church, one that would welcome and love them and would have the humility to receive from them their unique spiritual and cultural contributions.

When Pastor Petros and I met that first time, our hearts warmly linked. Our visions conspired toward the idea of every tribe, language, and nation in a local church.

Within a few weeks, we were baptizing nine Habesha (a word meaning "the People" in the Amharic language). They were mostly young adults with only one child among them. Ten precious and diverse new lives were added to our congregation that day.

For seven years, the afternoon Habesha fellowship met in another part of Cincinnati at a generously provided Salvation Army facility, having several different American home churches among their growing group. Then in the summer of 2004 they were looking for a new meeting room. We invited them to our campus in Uptown Cincinnati, and something extraordinary and special was underway.

Within two years, Jan and I would be invited to a vision-sharing meeting with the Habesha leaders. This would result in their decision to officially join then First Christian Assembly of God (our prior church name). The group had grown. They translated the church bylaws into Amharic, studied and agreed to the content, and then, on a Sunday morning with singing and rejoicing, twenty-seven adults and nine children officially joined our church body as members! This was in addition to the handful already woven together with us from that earlier 1997 baptism day.

The Habesha leaders moved the Amharic language service to Sunday mornings alongside one of our two English services so that their children could be included in the kids' ministries, and over time, the adults could matriculate into an English service and fuller engagement as one body.

Many years later now, over 150 Habesha adults, representing ninety-one language groups from back home, and a hundred children comprise 20 percent of Peoples Church Cincinnati. Women and men from among them serve on staff, on the deacon board, and in every ministry of the church for the whole congregation. And we still have an Amharic language service for the first-generation immigrants. After all, when John was shown the multitude gathered before the throne (Revelation 7:9), he saw the tribes, he heard their languages, and they were *one*.

Pastor Petros is the senior associate pastor to all of Peoples Church and the wisest leader among us.

Chapter 12

THE NEXT GENERATION

By late 2004, we were leaking out some of our long-term attenders. I wish I could say we were intentionally investing them into new church plants, which is different from "losing" people.

We were losing people.

The church was quaking a bit. We had experienced a lot of change over the past twelve months: new vision articulated, new staff members, new attenders and members, new languages in the halls and café—church change.

Under our young worship pastor, Jason Sharp, who'd grown up in the church, our music was now keyboard-based, more syncopated, and from diverse artists and songwriters. Sounds, sights, and smells (uniquely spicy aromas from the church kitchen some Sundays) throughout our church life were vibrant, diverse, and new.

"New" was challenging for some of our veterans in our nearly hundred-year-old church.

I remember an office visit by one of our seasoned leaders to tell me she knew of forty couples who would be leaving by new year 2005.

Another office appointment by two of the major donors in the church was for letting me know the worship needed to go back to "normal."

Finances were flagging. Attendance as well. We were down about 5 percent in both. At times, fear would grip my heart. Many nights included 2 a.m. sleeplessness and "carpet time" (prostrated prayer on the bedroom floor). Needling questions occupied my heart. Had I heard the Lord wrong? Was I wrecking the church? Was I leading us forward too fast?

Thanks to Him, our board and staff held steady in total unity. We thank the Lord that He helped Jan and me not to lead from fear or make bad decisions out of our anxieties but to servant-lead out of sound theology, ecclesiology, and the present, clear, and loving guidance of the Holy Spirit.

For sure we were making mistakes. At times I argued with oppositional people rather than just listening and inviting them to pray with us about what the Lord wanted.

At other times, I felt I was trying to perform heart surgery on our body with more of a blunt instrument than with the skillful use of a scalpel. Blunt instruments tend to crush and bruise. I had many one-on-one meetings that I wish I could have back and do differently.

For sure we could have led better.

One man left during that time telling me, "I know black people, and they want their own church. What you're trying to do won't work." Some years later he called back to say, "I see now you were right, Chris. But boy, you could have explained things a lot better."

He was right.

We saw something else happening, too, however.

As young people in the church grew up and joined the work, we saw indigenous leaders like Jason and Jen Sharp (the worship pastor and his wife) emerging to deepen and accelerate the vision, the calling of a reconciling church. Jason had a gift for playing and leading with his whole being and soul. He was unafraid to push the envelope and willing to tap the brakes as needed.

We trimmed the budget and "set our faces like a flint" (see Isaiah 50:7).

As 2005 began, forty couples *didn't* leave. Some did, but not forty. And one new couple came who brought relief as they joined our staff.

Tom Baxter had grown up at First Christian Assembly in the 1990s. He had listened intently to the theology laid down from Isaiah 58–61 and Luke 4 during those mid-90s preparation years, theology that profoundly rounded out our gospel understanding.

After being away for college and three years of youth ministry in another state, Tom brought his young family home to Cincinnati the week after Christmas 2004 to join the effort and lead the youth ministry. Jamie, his young Norwegian-descent wife from South Dakota, completed the package.

Together they would add so much strength to the rest of the team as part of the indigenous next-generation catalysts—with their talents, prayer lives, and insights now joining the rest of us—that we would never look back.

I'll never forget that year 2004. It is a year I'll be reflecting on for the rest of my life and mining for thanksgiving and worship (Psalm 77:11; 2 Timothy 1:3).

Chapter 13

TURNING THE CORNER

In 2005, the church began to grow.

We saw doctors, lawyers, and educators joining the vision. We also saw the Lord saving people recently out of prison, people with drug-addicted backgrounds, and folks from across the socioeconomic spectrum. Diverse inclusion was going to be at a whole new level. And in the midst of it all, the finances were regaining strength.

We would make it.

By 2006, we had become 15 percent racially/ethnically diverse, with 12 percent African American and 3 percent international. Considering our starting point of 98 percent Caucasian in 1995, we rejoiced!

We also realized we needed more. Church-like-heaven-on-earth was more than just a room of diverse people worshiping together, as dynamic and attractive as that is to pre-Christians. We should expect more.

For sure, we were seeing a lot of people come to the Lord. John 17:20-23 was proving itself: "Father, unite them so the world will believe" (my paraphrase). Internationals were visiting and staying because they saw black and white Christians loving one another, serving together, worshiping as one. Yet we sensed in our hearts that we had a long way to go to achieve the idea of being a reconciling church. In many respects, we were diverse but not at the more granular level of everyday life. Further, we were still far from being a demographic microcosm of our city.

What could we do?

Our 2006 board-and-staff retreat honed in on this question: What if our congregation reflected the city proper in demographics: 40 percent white, 40 percent black, and 20 percent international?

How prophetically would that speak to our city? How much glory would that bring to our King? How much richness and joy would that bring to our lives? What if our relationships were deep cross-racially, cross-ethnically, cross-economically, and cross-generationally? Deep. Not just "hello" and a hug on Sunday, but deep. Now that would be rich.

How would we get there?

Coming out of that retreat, we were on fire. God had spoken to our hearts, we could see some measurable goals, and we had a plan.

A flooring company CEO in our lead team and our executive pastor Brandon Wilkes (with an eight-year P&G career under his belt) offered to build a diverse team of women and men to prepare a strategic plan. Their plan hinged on an audacious element: a twenty-week-long small group experience of intentionally diverse participants led by trained pairs, one black and one white, facilitator teams using original curriculum developed in-house. To boot, the first two weeks would involve me vision-casting a future 40/40/20 (black/white/international) redemptive community worshiping at the geographic heart of our city, as well as laying down a biblical foundation and strategy and unpacking why diverse unity and the Great Commission are inextricably linked. Tall order. But *so* exciting! The goals included going deeper relationally—not as measurable as attendance demographics but an important new heart-level priority for us.

Two hundred eighty adults began in these Vision Experience groups, eighty more than we had hoped. Twenty weeks later, 220 people completed with a culminating experience at the National Underground Railroad Freedom Center on the Ohio River, the Civil War-era Mason-Dixon Line. The completion number astounded and excited us. This was a critical mass for helping us to move forward more deeply, more authentically reconciling, more richly enjoying and including each other fully in one another's lives.

The curriculum team had compellingly made the case that racial reconciliation through the gospel of Jesus Christ was essential for the American church to live out John 17 and its implications. We were reaching a tipping point of forward energy and unity.

Our church would never be the same.

THE GOSPEL OF JESUS CHRIST, MISSIONS, AND BIBLICAL JUSTICE

For a hundred years our church, as we saw it, had been all about the gospel—making disciples, planting new churches, and serving in international missions.

Now as we grew diversely, we realized there was more to believing, living, and spreading the gospel of Jesus Christ.

The gospel required more of us than we had understood. Jesus had shown us more during His earthly ministry than we were believing and doing. In our former mono-ethnic, homogeneously cultured church, we simply couldn't see all that He was about. Our perspectives were limited, and we didn't know it.

For years, we had already appreciated that the gospel was making headway toward the easily measurable list of Unreached People Groups (Joshua-Project.net), answering the call to "make disciples of *all* peoples" (Matthew 28:18-20).

Obviously, international missions efforts to spread the gospel were essential for fulfilling the call to "make disciples of all *peoples [ethnae]."*

Not to work toward that target seemed spiritually immature and short-sighted to us. So did the idea of not evangelizing in our own city, our own country. Clearly, the gospel called us to reach our neighbor. But now, "our neighbor" included all our neighbors, not just those like us. So our under-standing of neighbor, and peoples, was being challenged. Both now included proximity folk unlike us. That was what was new.

Something else new, and visceral, was happening in us as well: a recognition that the full effect of the gospel must include justice, biblical justice—a marked increase of Kingdom life and principles directly and tangibly affecting human realities, societal structures, and unjust histories that were un-Kingdom like, while at the same time not surrendering any emphasis on the evangelization of individuals.

As who we were as a church now included diverse believers from variegated personal and group experiences, we were beginning to understand that discipleship of diverse people required us to incorporate more than making sure new believers acquired Bible knowledge and more than just teaching spiritual disciplines, as important as they are. No, discipleship would also include "teaching them to obey *everything*" that Jesus commanded.

And from Jesus' own use of Isaiah 61 in His inaugural vision recorded in Luke 4, it was inescapable that offering healing to broken hearts, setting captives free, and ministering to the poor in addition to Good News proclamation was integral to Jesus' anointing and mission. How had we missed these dimensions?

For us, this now meant that some of the young black men coming to Christ in our church needed more than a new believers' class or a one-to-one discipler, though they needed that, too. They would need someone to get involved in the matters of life that had shackled them from their youth on, and for some of them, this had been so for generations. In addition to knowing how to love and know the Lord and His Word, they would need healing for the racial sins against them. They would need help disentangling from an unfair legal system that had so disproportionately targeted them with stiffer penalties for the same crimes that wealthier white youth went free on—something that had been going on in our city for decades.

For us, the mission of the gospel in our community would now include coming alongside the at-risk urban elementary schools in our city, where generationally poor and fatherless kids were still largely illiterate and math deficient.

Now the mission of the gospel, and true religion that our Father would find pure and faultless, would not only include keeping ourselves from being polluted morally by a decadent world (James 1:27b), but also would include taking care of foster kids and single moms in their distress (James 1:27a).

Now our work would include seeking to understand the snarls and snares of an unwieldy and unaccountable immigration system, where often the right hand didn't understand what the left hand was doing. As a result, life was very messy for so many of our people now in the Lord and in the church.

Because for so long we had practiced homogeneous, ethnically, and economically siloed church, we simply had never personally or corporately felt the fullness of the gospel call. Now we found that a diversely united church opened our minds and our hearts to the fullness of what the gospel had always been about.

My, how things were changing for us.

Chapter 15

AWAKENINGS

In early 2006, Taft Elementary, our neighborhood public school in Uptown Cincinnati, was slated to close soon. Taft was in abject academic failure. Only 130 students remained in a school that had flourished with 400 in its prime decades before.

For several years we had attempted relationship, but the suburban-background, Caucasian principal wouldn't accept our requests for a meeting. From where we stood, he seemed holed up in his office, literally. His overwhelmingly African American student population came from families living well below the poverty line. He was a fish out of water and seemed not to recognize help when it was staring him in the face.

Then after a leadership change at Taft, we tried again. This time it was a success! The new principal, a Muslim woman of African American ethnicity, opened the school wide to us. On the Saturday before the 2006-2007 school year was to begin, she invited us onto the property for a workday. Over a hundred volunteers fanned out across the school campus to spread fresh mulch and plant new flowers, repaint and repair the playground that had gone unused for years, paint and pray over all the classrooms, and fill 150 school backpacks for every student's first day of school.

The church was so excited. The story fueled so much energy in our worship, our preaching, and our altar calls. Many new guests were captivated by the stories of Taft Elementary's turnaround over the next few years. If the gospel included the church intentionally loving at-risk kids, they were in! Within five or six years, the student population was over three hundred. They were out of academic failure, and they were holding their annual sixth grade promotions every spring in our sanctuary.

As of this writing, they still do.

Chapter 16

FULL CIRCLE

I still remember when I realized who he was. Terry Thomas had begun to attend our services and gave his life to the Lord. He was Timothy's younger brother, the same Timothy who'd been killed as an unarmed teen in the police shooting in early 2001.

Terry had found Christ . . . and a church home.

Racially reconciling church was working to draw people to Jesus in the most promising ways.

Over the next two years, the mother of his three kids gave her life to the Lord as well, and they were both baptized. One by one, the children surrendered their lives to Jesus, too.

Terry and Otisz had never seen a marriage on either side of their family tree. Mentored by a seasoned Christian couple in the church, and with support from many different leaders, black, white, and brown, Terry and 'Tiz were married in 2011. We rejoiced!

We were witnessing in real time, in real lives, the promises of Isaiah 61:3-4 come to pass: "They will be called oaks of righteousness, the planting of the LORD, that He may be glorified. . . . They will repair the ruined cities, the desolations of many generations" (NASB).

Discipleship in the midst of generational brokenness is never easy, never without a mix of forward and backward steps, but we were rejoicing that the full gospel that reconciles sinners to the Father and divided people to each other was dynamically and profoundly at work. This gospel of reconciliation was bringing us redemptively full circle to the "binding of the brokenhearted" (Isaiah 61:1-3) with salvation and healing taking place in the extended family of the very man shot by the police in 2001, which had sparked our Cincinnati riots, right at the beginning of our journey into this reconciling vision.

Only God. Only *this gospel.*

Chapter 17

ORPHANS

In late 2007, God was stirring something new for us.

By now he had taken us deeply into His heart for racial reconciliation through the gospel. Likewise, He had compelled us to welcome the stranger, the refugee, and the immigrant "foreigner." All were welcome to the miracle of the Cross and being included into the body of Jesus at our church.

Yet until now, we had never lifted the cause of the fatherless. Not really.

Our ten core values included justice, underscored by Psalm 82:3-4, "Defend the weak and the fatherless; uphold the cause of the poor and the oppressed. Rescue the weak and the needy; deliver them from the hand of the wicked."

We were in many ways pressing into biblical justice, Psalm 82-type stuff—our Taft Elementary work, elements of racial and immigrant justice, upholding various causes. But what about the foster care kids in our city? Our Cincinnati foster care program was in crisis.

The content of James 1:27 was beginning to quicken my heart. "Religion that God our Father accepts as pure and faultless is this: to look after orphans and widows in their distress and to keep oneself from being polluted by the world."

What captivated me from the passage was the way James linked personal holiness and societal righteousness as together providing pure, faultless religion. Wow! How had the American church allowed these two biblical emphases—personal righteousness and societal justice—to get so bifurcated in our minds?

The enemy of the gospel had really hoodwinked the church. As a result, people in society were suffering. Children were suffering. Single moms were suffering. Black and brown people were oppressed. Generations had been devastated.

For a spring sermon series in 2008, we planned "Orphan," and we would just go right at the topic for three weeks, unpacking the Word.

What I personally still needed, though, was to understand the status of vulnerable kids in my city. A laywoman in our church asked if I would meet a fellow pastor whose heart and life were also stirred with vision for the orphan. Neither of them knew about the sermon series our team was already planning. It was just God prompting them concurrently.

Larry Bergeron lit me on fire. He shared basic foster care information I simply didn't know. "Chris, nationally over 500,000 kids are in the foster system. In our city there are nearly two thousand. Because of licensed family shortages, 35 percent of our kids are sent to other Ohio cities for care, often hours away, but still have to return weekly to Cincinnati for bio-parent, medical, and court visits."

I was astounded but, at the same time, ignited.

Our church needed to know. The church of Cincinnati needed to know.

Chapter 18

COLLECTIVE IMPACT

Diversely uniting our local church was changing how I thought about the collective church in the city. If the local church needed to be a better reflection of Jesus' blood purchase—every tribe, language, and nation—ought not also a regional church be more united?

It was the concluding Sunday of the "Orphan" series, March 2008.

As I shared the citywide need, my heart stirred with a vision Larry Bergeron had spoken to me, "What if every church in Greater Cincy wrapped around one mobilized family to welcome a foster child? We would have more families than kids needing a safe family."

Larry and his wife were listening from the back of the room during our service that day; they came to observe and pray over fruit from his labor, a mobilized me. We were excited. God was touching the hearts of our congregation.

When I walked off the stage and sat down next to John Pepper, retired P&G CEO, he pulled on my shirt and said, "Chris, that was an amazing vision you spoke. I'd like my son to meet you." David was serving as a Hamilton County commissioner. Our city's Children's Services fell under his oversight.

Within a month we met. Larry Bergeron joined us, and David Pepper included Moira Weir, head of Job and Family Services that housed the foster care system for Greater Cincinnati's biggest county, Hamilton County, and oversaw state responsibility for twelve hundred children.

In that meeting, as Larry shared his heart and the data in his head, Moira asked about the church he led. Were they fostering? Were they adopting?

His answer floored us all. Yes, there were twenty-nine fostered and adopted children in the church.

We asked if it would be a strength to her team if church groups were signing up to complete the thirty-eight hours of foster training. She hesitated but answered that she'd never seen that before. Within a year, church-based trainings were taking place, some with thirty and forty people, some with seventy and eighty.

A Coalition of Care (coalitionofcare.org) had been born, and it started through formerly unaligned local churches uniting in response to the cries of the fatherless. Church-like-heaven-on earth was taking on additional meaning for me.

Chapter 19

CROSSONOMICS

As our church grew in racial richness, we also grew in nations inclusion. As we increased in color and ethnic diversity, we also began to see economic/class inclusion soaring.

Early in our planning, praying, and dreaming for a John 17 church, we anticipated that our economic mix would change.

It did, in fact, but not as we expected. Yes, people of lower income, or no income, were joining the family (including homeless and mentally ill people with no disposable cash), but so were CEOs, doctors, and lawyers—educated people of means drawn to Jesus' inspiring vision of a Revelation 5:9 church and the societal change it promises.

Our incredible people-mix of languages and skin hues, of immigrants, and of rich and poor was learning to love one another from the heart through Christ in us. So much hard work remained, however, to realize our full potential, so we embarked on creating Vision Experience 2.0. We would call it Crossonomics.

Again, a team of leaders, this time led by Oneya Okuwobi, worked to prepare a Scripture-rooted small group curriculum that would look at "The Cross and Economics." What does the Bible have to say about the rich and the poor as one body together?

What we discovered was powerful. From 1 Corinthians 11 to the whole book of James, we realized that God's heart for diversely united *ekklesia* (church) meant not only the color and culture separation being erased, but also the socioeconomic divide.

At the end of our eight-week churchwide Crossonomics experience, we would never be the same. God opened our hearts in new ways to see profound value in one another and to embrace all our gifts.

A poignant moment came later when we vision-cast the idea of eliminating our mortgage. I invited those interested in hearing a strategy to join me for a short meeting after the second service. On my way through the lobby, I was stopped sequentially by two different regular attenders: the first a sometimes homeless man with mental illness, and the second a CEO of a good-sized company. The first man pressed a ragged dollar bill into my hand and said, "Here, pastor, this is for the mortgage." I thanked him; my eyes teared. I hugged him and moved on a few more steps when a second man in the lobby humbly pulled me aside. He mentioned he couldn't attend the meeting, but that he and his wife were in for $100,000. I was stunned. Both at the size of that pledge and at the rapid, odd sequence I had just experienced—the obedience of the first man to give from his lack and then that being matched within three walking strides by a similarly generous gift from the couple of means.

When I arrived at the classroom for the meeting, I wrote $100,001 on a whiteboard and thanked the Lord out loud with tears that the first two donations were already in.

Within a few short months, we were mortgage-free. I'll never forget the combined first two gifts toward that effort.

Indeed, God was teaching me—teaching us all—that the Ephesians 2:15 church, one new humanity through the power of the Cross, was going to be a new kind of incredible for all of us.

Chapter 20

WE WERE NOT ALONE

In 2011, we joined a multiethnic church cohort by Leadership Network, a nationally recognized leadership collaborative for pastors and churches. This particular experience was designed as a mutual learning and strategic planning process with twelve multiethnic church leadership teams coming together in Dallas for two days, four times, over eighteen months for facilitated group processes and best-practice discussions. What a priceless validation it became for us.

Some of us in the cohort had been friends for years, but special new friendships also formed. Here we all were, part of the first such cohort nationally as far as we knew, but more significantly, the group included fellow travelers years deep into this refresh work of biblical church.

Not only were we encouraged by one another's successes, we drew comfort from the failures and weaknesses. We were not alone!

I experienced many key moments throughout the cohort, but two were absolutely crucial.

The first was when Derwin Grey of Transformation Church, and former NFL defensive back, stepped toward me from his seat during a peer review of our church's strategic plans. With intense love and obvious disbelief, he asked, "How long did you say you are taking to facilitate your church name-change process?!"

"Three to five years," I mumbled.

"How long have you been there, Chris?" quizzed Derwin.

"Ten years as lead, and eighteen total on staff," I revealed.

"Man, you need to take like six months and start moving now."

Strangely, that same summer we were in an inexplicable financial lull. The church was growing again after Crossonomics whittled us down some, just as had The Vision Experience a few years before, but now we were growing through summer itself. Yet the funds were low—and not normal summer low. A $100,000 deficit had opened up, 10 percent of our annual, general fund.

Here's what was at issue. A good two years earlier while on a solitary prayer retreat, I had heard the Lord speak plainly to me how He wanted the name "Peoples Church" in place of First Christian Assembly of God. We would still belong to the Assemblies of God (AG) network within which I serve on a statewide leadership level, but our name was now to express His Revelation 7:9 vision.

I had argued with Him about it. "Lord, it's costly to make these changes. We've come a long way, Lord, why don't we spread all this change out a little more?"

Now Pastor Derwin Gray was in my face. In love.

Chapter 21

———————

FIRST LOVE

Sometime after returning to Cincinnati from that two-day cohort, I stepped into a small Wednesday night corporate prayer meeting weighed down by the financial deficit burden. Near the meeting end, I asked those gathered to be praying with church leadership about our financial situation. One elderly woman of God, Theodora, a woman of color, mentioned afterward that she believed we were supposed to ask Him, "Why are we in this pinch?"

I agreed. "Let's pray on that very question and connect again Sunday," I reservedly responded.

That Sunday I was away and Pastor Tom Baxter texted me: "Theodora says, 'First Love' . . . ???"

Really, Lord? You and me? We're out of sync? It didn't make sense to me at the time. My abiding times with the Lord were rich. I believed my heart was surrendered under Him. I thought that maybe Theodora just "missed it." And why hadn't the Lord spoken to me?

Later that week, I experienced that 2 a.m. wakeup call to prayer—the one where you just know to get out of bed and seek the Lord's face. In my spirit, I could feel I was to lie prostrate, face down before the Lord in prayer. As I did so, I heard the Lord prompt me to read Revelation 2, the "first love" passage.

As my Bible app glowed up into my face from the dark floor, I scrolled on my phone to the right spot as I was prayerfully propped up on my elbows before the Lord. I noticed it was Jesus' letter to the church at Ephesus. That got my attention.

Each verse resonated with me until that well-known spot. "You have persevered and have endured hardships for my name. . . .Yet I hold this against you:You have forsaken the love you had at first." In the recently new at that time 2011 NIV, the words were different than the "first love" words I had grown up with. Again I asked Him, "You and me, Lord?"

"No," I heard in my spirit, "keep reading," and I sensed Him telling me, "You're no longer doing the things you did in the beginning." Wow. Oh my. I felt a nudge to turn to Ephesians 1 and read.

Still "on my face" before the Lord, I read down to verse 15. Paul was commending the Ephesian church for their love, their love for *all* God's people. It's as if He's saying, "I affirm you for your love, not just for the other believers like yourselves, but for those unlike you also. I affirm you for your love for *all* the people." As we discussed in Part One, Ephesians 2 presses out this interpretation.

So in Revelation 2, the Lord is "care-fronting" the Ephesian church for losing the love they had at the beginning, for not doing the things they used to do. He was correcting them for losing the love required for a diversely united church, for the mystery of Christ's unity announced in Ephesians 3:6.

Like a train rolling through my being, I heard the Lord say, "I gave you something to do. Lead a church name-change process, from First Christian Assembly of God (our name for the prior seventy-five of one hundred years) to Peoples Church, and to get back to the work of aggressively seeking racial reconciliation and justice in the church, the city, and the nation."

Repentance flooded my heart. What the Lord had tasked me with on my 2009 prayer retreat had been placed to the side out of transition fatigue and personal complacency.

At the time, the Lord had so unmistakably given me the name Peoples Church, He had even been so specific as to confirm to me it was okay not to include an apostrophe.

I remember on that 2009 prayer retreat being inspired by People's Church Oklahoma City's story. I even later phoned Pastor Herbert Cooper to seek his blessing to adopt the name, just without the apostrophe. He graciously let me know that no blessing was needed and that he had no ownership on the name. Still, it felt right to request his blessing as it was his story that God used to prompt all of this in me.

The morning after that pivotal prayer and visioning retreat, God used the newspaper in my driveway to help seal the deal, and then I was too malingering and didn't follow through. In the driveway, I asked the Lord again about the apostrophe as I was picking up the newspaper. As it slipped out of the thin, plastic sleeve, it opened to a front page headline about Peoples Bank, no apostrophe. I smiled and said, "Okay, Lord."

Until it wasn't.

That evening at the kitchen table, I felt myself backpedaling over dinner when I shared the name with my family. My kids said, "I don't know, Dad." The staff and board reacted the same way, even tossing out other new name ideas! No one was nostalgically committed to First Christian Assembly of God, necessarily. Many even in the church couldn't remember that name correctly!

To the younger generation, the FCA name seemed arrogant and complex. Why would a church call itself "first" anything (I know, there were historical reasons, but they no longer communicated well). Very few in our city could recognize the church by its wordy name, except some from older generations.

Yet I felt zero synergy from others for the name "Peoples Church" as I lobbed it out there to my intimate inner circles of family, friends, and co-workers. So, I backed up and set it aside.

Now, two years later, our finances were on life support, God had said "first love" through Theodora, and I was on the floor at 2:00 a.m. reading Revelation 2 and Ephesians 1.

And God was speaking.

Chapter 22

THE NAME CHANGE

Two a.m. carpet time is not all that unusual when leading spiritual change, church change, Kingdom risky business. Satan hates us when we're pressing out the gospel of the Kingdom of God. And the Lord also uses the wee hours of the morning to speak or call us to deeper prayer, deeper revelations of Himself and His agenda.

Lying there on my stomach next to my bed propped on my elbows, repentance flooding my heart, I cried out, "How, Lord, how?"

"Chris, just tell them the story of how I gave you the name. I'll take care of the rest." And boy, did He. Within six months.

First, I shared with my family, the staff, and the board the exact story, my heart and what I had heard from God two years earlier about the name, Peoples Church. From my kids to senior deacons they all said, "Why didn't you tell us that before? This is a no-brainer. That's the name."

I was astounded.

The board asked me to tell the story at our November business meeting. After I did, the board asked me to tell the rest of the church at our weekend services.

I knew the congregation wouldn't react with 100 percent joy , and they didn't. The vote the next April was hardly sterling at 77 percent in favor. But the name passed.

We were now Peoples Church—and within nine months of Derwin's catalytic challenge.

Still Pentecostal. Still in the Assemblies of God network. Still biblically evangelical. Still rooted in Scripture and theologically conservative—maybe more now than ever, especially if being biblically conservative means aligning with the Word regardless how that looks or sounds to a partisan world.

Chapter 23

CHRIST COVETS NATIONAL STAGE

A part of the story I skipped was this: Just a few months before the name-change vote, while relaxing at my in-laws house over the New Year's holiday 2012, I remember how stunned I felt when I opened the front section of the *Cincinnati Enquirer* on their family room coffee table.

"Christ Covets National Stage," it read. What? (You can search for the story online at Cincinnati.com.)

I soon realized the subject was Christ Hospital's expansion vision, but nonetheless, my spirit was also seeing that headline prophetically. Smiling to myself as I began to read the article, the blood drained from my face as I realized the Lord really was up to something with this headline.

Not only was the hospital growing, but its expansion was taking place directly across the street from our church campus, and *how* it was coming to pass deeply resonated with my heart.

A trio of Cincinnati businessmen were collaborating to create investment opportunities for middle- and working-class African Americans in our city. Wealth creation through development projects had long been a pathway for increasing assets for so many in our city's history. With only a few exceptions, blacks were never included at the table. This new project, however, shouting the name Christ on the front page of the newspaper, would be different.

Further, the acquisition of two properties directly across Taft Road from where we owned four hundred feet of prime frontage, with scant parking behind our facilities, would include tearing down an eyesore building and converting the surface into two hundred parking spaces!

Certain Peoples Church folk had been praying for twenty years that we could purchase that property, tear down the decaying facility, and turn the space into parking. Now, Christ was doing it! Christ Hospital.

Instantly, a thousand thoughts flurried through my mind. How would I get on these men's schedules? For two reasons: one, to hear and understand the smart, innovative vision to engender African American wealth creation (African Americans have on average a net worth one twelfth of that of Caucasian Americans); and two, to see if we could possibly gain Sunday use of the new parking!

Within weeks, I was meeting with one of the three. Dan Ruh was a young businessman new in Christ through a church we had helped plant some fifteen years earlier. What a joy to hear his testimony and see downline fruit from having invested key leaders and funds to open a new church to reach people that no one was reaching. Crossroads Church was on fire and growing quickly through gospel conversions.

Dan shared with me the gist of the three men's mutual vision. He encouraged me to get on the schedules of the other two for my other questions: How did the idea come about? How would it work? With whom could I talk about the parking?

Next was Albert Smitherman. Albert owned a leading concrete and construction firm in our city. Jostin's was leading the way for employing second-chance citizens and was still one of only a few African American–owned development companies. Albert's parents had instilled in him a vision for giving people a hand up, especially people of color who hadn't had the same opportunities as he had. Albert's father was Proctor & Gamble Company's first PhD scientist of color. What a heritage.

I knew Albert's wife, Liza, from serving jointly on the board of Cincinnati's rescue mission, City Gospel Mission. Unquestionably, this couple was centered on spending their lives for the sake of others. Albert and I would fast become friends for life. This man had so much to teach me. He had conceived the idea of bundle investing for acquiring properties to be developed then leased and sold. Bundle investing would allow an investor to invest $100,000 by combining ("bundling") twenty or more smaller investments from family and friends. The initial property purchase would be owned by these investors then flipped to a larger investor after development and successful leasing, tripling the initial investments. Then, repeat.

Brilliant.

But who could help me with the parking? Albert pointed me to Christ Hospital's Chief Operating Officer, the third individual pictured in that January 2 front page story with Dan and Albert.

Easier said than done.

Weeks, then months, went by without access to this man. I was growing discouraged.

Chapter 24

CONVERGENCE

With the name change complete and new business cards in our pockets, Brandon Wilkes and I entered the conference room at Christ Hospital for our appointment with James Gray, Chief Operating Officer.

The first minutes began quite awkwardly. Jim's opening line, before even sitting down with us was, "You need to know I'm an avid atheist, and you have eleven minutes." Oh. That's why he hadn't accepted my appointment requests all spring. Why would a local church reach out for time on his crazy busy schedule?

My response, as I slid my new Peoples Church card across the table, was, "What you need to know is . . . I'm here to talk about your parking."

He hesitated and then gently laughed, and we all relaxed. Then he picked up and studied the card. Looking at Brandon and me, black and white, this not-yet-believing Euro-descent, gay man asked, "And what's the significance of this name?"

"Well, our church is about racial reconciliation—ethnic and economic inclusion. We believe the gospel of Jesus Christ is for everyone. So is our church."

He studied my face. He studied Brandon. He looked at us both, back and forth. Then he sat down.

"Ok, let's talk about the parking." Within ten minutes, something better than we could have hoped for, better than we had ever prayed for, was completed. We would be permitted free use of the lot on Sundays, provided we were careful no cars stayed overnight.

Then, strikingly, Jim looked at me and sincerely said, "I like you. We should have beers and talk theology." I was stunned. The evangelist in me was intrigued and thankful for the invitation.

Before long we were meeting at a bar over a Diet Coke and a Stella to share life, hearts, and, in time, theology: an avid atheist and an avid lover of Jesus.

Within six months, I was suggesting Dietrich Bonhoeffer's, *The Cost of Discipleship*, and this profoundly intellectual, well-read, and spiritually yearning man accepted that challenge.

God has an amazing way of working. And Christ indeed was preparing a national stage for His vision of diversely united local churches. Way more than we could imagine.

Chapter 25

THE *LOS ANGELES TIMES,*
100 YEARS AFTER AZUSA

Only one week after our name change vote had passed in April 2012, an *L.A. Times* reporter attended a Sunday morning service at Peoples. Purely coincidental timing with the name change? I don't think so. God was orchestrating and beginning to highlight the Revelation 7:9 church to our church and the nation on an expanding stage.

The journalist was captivated by the rich racial and ethnic diversity of our church. That Sunday, he observed a vibrant, Spirit-pulsating worship service. He freely talked with people before and after services. Sure, he was thinking about 2012 politics and Ohio's role in them. But we were thinking about a different Kingdom and were glad he was seeing a glimpse of it, not only in our church but also in the several others he studied for his piece.

Nearly 105 years earlier in 1907, an *L.A. Times* writer had visited the Azusa Street Mission, a multiracial gathering of Pentecostal believers worshiping under black leadership, William J. and Jennie Seymour. Only that reporter came away nauseated at what he described as a "disgraceful intermingling of the races."

Now this 2012 reporter was seeing a downstream influence of Seymour and seemed intrigued by the implications for our society.

An important part of our church story was that a woman leader named Nancy Starrett had visited Azusa in our second year of formal existence, 1907. On her return, the church embraced a fuller experience of the Holy

Spirit in the Christian life and would never be the same. God had used African American leadership for our local church, and the worldwide church at large, way back then.

Now, just weeks after our name change, the rich diversity of Peoples Church was nationally highlighted on the front page of the *Los Angeles Times*. (You can find the story online at latimes.com, titled "Obama could have a prayer among Ohio's white evangelicals.") Only Jesus, the Head of His church, could have orchestrated this. How else could this be explained?

Diversely united, gospel-centered congregations have influence far beyond their numbers. And the Lord was just beginning to show this to be true.

PART III

In the months that followed, Jesus increased the stage for church-like-heaven-on-earth thinking.

———————

Chapter 26

GROUND ZERO, ISRAEL, AND THE WEST BANK

Wherever Paul lifts up the one new humanity vision in the New Testament, he particularly zeroes in on uniting Jews and Greeks. They hated each other. But in Christ, things were to be different. In Christ not only are people reconciled to the Father but also to each other. "We regard no one from a worldly point of view" (2 Corinthians 5:16). For Paul, this was a key apologetic, as it was for John as evidenced in John 17:20-23.

An invitation to attend a Middle East Christian conference, Christ at the Checkpoint in the West Bank, hosted by Bethlehem Bible College (whom our church had financially supported for many years), sparked in me the idea of Ephesians 2:15b being literal, "His purpose was to create in himself one new humanity out of the two, thus making peace."

What if there were a reconciling movement among believers in the Holy Land between Jewish and Palestinian followers of Jesus? Could the work of Ephesians 2:15 get any more literal today? Perhaps if the effort were somehow with Greeks and Israelis, but that's not where the deepest Jew/Gentile church fracture today is. It's in the West Bank/Gaza and Israel.

Believers live just a few miles apart but have never met one another. They fear one another. They are more captive to the larger geopolitical realities than to the gospel, but what if that were different? Even just among a few of them? What kind of spiritual breakthrough could this cause in the heavenlies over the land and in the earth?

In 2012, a few of us traveled to Bethlehem with this reflection percolating in our hearts.

For nearly fifteen years by then, Peoples Church had financially supported Bethlehem Bible College—the primary gospel-rooted, evangelical/Pentecostal training institution for Palestinian believers called into vocational ministry, pastoring, and missions.

At the same time in Cincinnati, we cherished a long-standing relationship with the Messianic Jewish community. Rabbis Michael and Rachel Wolf were like James among us in the church of Cincinnati, lead elders of wisdom as James was for the early church in Jerusalem.

Surely there were messianic leaders in Israel who would similarly be captivated with a biblical vision of church reconciliation, diverse believers' unity, Jew and Gentile, in the Holy Land? And there are.

But this work is not easy and has so far to go. The tensions of life in the West Bank/Israel and how the Bible is interpreted by some believers in Israel/Palestine make it difficult.

An intentional, Spirit-led diverse group would have to set their hearts on the power of what this could mean for the worldwide church, much less for those living in the Holy Land itself. Worldly points of view would have to be laid aside. The Kingdom of God would have to be considered primary as the starting *and* ending point.

The trip to Bethlehem in 2012 uncovered some hesitant beginnings, but beginnings. Seeds were already being planted there. Indigenous leaders in the Holy Land, on both sides, have reconciliation in their hearts. Pray for vision, practical leadership, and a reconciled church in the land of the Bible.

One new humanity church in the Middle East would change things.

Chapter 27

ST. LOUIS (FERGUSON)

Steve Pike was leading the Church Multiplication Network (CMN) for the Assemblies of God (AG). We both have Colorado roots.

We had long been friends and often had discussed God's heart for racial reconciliation and a vision of planting gospel-centered churches that lived three-dimensionally in their cities as proclamation and demonstration embassies of the Kingdom of God. These churches worked transformatively for both individual salvation and societal righteousness (Isaiah 58–61). And they succeeded in being racially and ethnically inclusive and celebratory, in the name and for the fame of Jesus, in the power of the Spirit, teaching new disciples to obey everything He taught (Matthew 28:20), not just belief without these deep works.

Over coffee at a conference one day in early 2012, I felt prompted in my spirit to ask Steve a question: What could happen if CMN led the way in just such a vision for all the church, not just the AG, but including the AG? Steve's passion, and soon to be fruitfulness, was for four hundred to five hundred new churches a year.

What if these were tethered into a theological bedrock for church-like-heaven-on-earth and were trained in the principles and the practical steps to take? What if from his CMN platform Steve were to influence our greater body toward the richness of our original racial unity roots at Azusa Street? What if this could help inspire diversely united congregations in the church at large?

Steve was stirred. He said we would need a national voice to help us within the AG. "What about Scott Hagan?" I asked. Scott was pastoring a church he had planted in northern California. He had also earlier in his ministry successfully transitioned an historic homogeneous white church and had twice now successfully planted multiethnic congregations. Few people in our AG network articulate the vision better.

Soon after my return from Israel and the West Bank that spring, we held a four-way call with Scott and Michael Nelson. Nelson was president of the AG National Black Fellowship, which exists to empower African American pastors in their ministries and all AG churches toward racial reconciliation and inclusion.

With typical passion and vivacity, Scott leaned into the subject. "We need more key people," he said. "Let's do the talk again, but this time each of us invite three more leaders onto the call."

The next conference call included key leaders of color, Mark DeYmaz of Mosaix Global Network, and several AG national office holders. There was traction. Scott then encouraged us to hold this important discussion in an all-day face-to-face meeting. What if we all came to St. Louis together later that summer?

We did.

Out of that meeting of younger and older leaders—black, white and brown—emerged two crucial asks of our national fellowship: (1) Could we write a resolution that would rehearse for this current generation the repentance history regarding the role racism had played in our founding? And could we make a permanent seat for an African American on our national board at the same time? (2) Could we set up a standing committee to give guidance to the national network on theology and praxis for the multiethnic church?

Steve Pike and Malcolm Burleigh would submit the requests to our ELT (Executive Leadership Team) of six. (In late 2017, Malcolm would become the second African American ever elected to the ELT.)

The net result of this effort, after a new national multiethnic team of men and women came together under AG General Secretary Jim Bradford, was that the AG National Black Fellowship forwarded the history review resolution and national board (the Executive Presbytery) position. The effort took some time and careful, timely leadership by Michael Nelson and Walter Harvey, but eventually the envisioned resolution passed with unanimous acclamation in 2015. As a result, in 2017 not only was Malcolm elected U.S. Missions Director, but Sam Huddleston was elected to the newly minted African American Executive Presbyter seat. Permanent African American inclusion was secured at the highest board of a group whose origins had been inspired under black pastoral leader William J. Seymour.

We wouldn't get the standing committee to assist our churches and state-level teams around this multiethnic and multieconomic model yet, but racially inclusive leadership was secured at the national level.

Ethnic and racial inclusion require intentional effort, the help of the Holy Spirit, minority and majority group shared leadership, creative and shared initiative (shared ownership), and follow-through. When vision and direction are only majority group-initiated, the work suffers for lack of equitable, credible, diverse unity.

St. Louis was soon to experience Michael Brown's death and the ensuing reactions by the African American community in Ferguson and across the nation. But it was also a host city of a crucial meeting for spurring one another on to love and good works through Christ in us. He is tearing down the dividing walls of hostility (Ephesians 2:14).

Chapter 28

GLOBAL CHURCH IMPLICATIONS

(ONE UNITED INCLUSIVE AND INDIGENOUS CHURCH)

In the spring of 2013, another Peoples Church dream was coming together. Imagine if the leadership of the Egypt Assemblies of God and the sub-Saharan AG connected for strategic partnership with each other (something not seen before), and together with the American churches (Latin and North), joined hearts, talents, and gifts for reaching unreached peoples in North Africa, the Middle East, and Central Asia? And what if European and Asian believers joined the effort, teaming on purpose under the banner of the gospel to make disciples of every people from every people and include them in the growing church-like-heaven-on-earth?

Picture highly Islamicized nations of North Africa, the Middle East, and Central Asia receiving the benefit of multinational teams of believers bent on planting among them the fullness of the gospel of Jesus Christ together. "By your love for each other, your diverse unity, they will know that I am the Messiah" (John 17:20-23, my paraphrase). Just imagine taking Jesus seriously on this, knowing it has to be *unlikely love, unlikely unity* to be compelling enough to cause much of the far-from-Jesus world to believe—love across societal rifts that no one believes are bridgeable.

For one, there would have to be North African and sub-Saharan church connections.

Chapter 29

ELEVENTH-HOUR HARVESTERS

Before completing the Egypt/sub-Saharan connection story, I need to back up a few years.

When we were first thinking of church as "everybody in," we reflected on global missions. I remember learning that southern hemisphere Christianity was numerically far surpassing the north-of-the-equator crowd. Our Peoples Church missions board had long wondered why we weren't seeing more of a total church, inclusive church, effort toward finishing the task of every people, tribe, and language for which Jesus had paid with His blood.

Was this a matter of unintentional northern hemisphere exclusion of our southern hemisphere family from the task of global evangelization, a lack of southern hemisphere church vision and resources, or both? In addition, ethnic Americans were also largely missing from global missions work. What was this costing the global church effort toward completion of the Great Commission? By how much was it slowed? What talents, insights, abilities, and energy were missing from the global work of the church as a result?

In the early 2000s, I'd been invited into an emerging effort called Africa's Hope. Africa was experiencing explosive gospel growth, but more leaders were needed. Africa's Hope was an initiative to train sub-Saharan leaders to work the harvest, conserve the harvest, and keep the harvest theologically sound.

Before sending me to the Florida meeting, however, our church team needed to know if any Africans would be present—that it would not be just a bunch of white leaders trying to solve an African challenge without

African partnership. Yes, Lazarus Chakwera of Malawi would be there. A pastor, a seasoned man of the Kingdom, the national AG leader of Malawi, and the president of the entire Africa Assemblies of God Alliance (AAGA).

I couldn't wait to meet him.

Over lunch with Pastor Lazarus, I shared my questions, my heart, and my burden about the whole church taking the whole gospel into the whole world. I shared my misgivings about this enterprise, which seemed to me to be an almost all-white missions initiative, Africa's Hope, in the sub-Saharan context. Was this training effort invited? Was it falling under African spiritual authority? Was there co-equal visioning and sharing of the work? The answers were all yes. I was relieved and encouraged. But Lazarus understood my "young lion" questions and affirmed the caution, care, and representational humility underneath these thoughts.

He explained two things: First, the Gospel of Matthew records Jesus' parable about the harvesters who come late to the work, at the eleventh hour even, getting the same pay as the workers who had worked all day (Matthew 20). Pastor Lazarus turned this passion into missions training for leaders across Africa, called the "Eleventh Hour Institute." I was moved to the core of my heart. What a penetratingly smart way to think about global missions from the global south church, which was now beginning to rise up to initiate and participate in world missions.

Second, he expressed something else in his Oklahoman English drawl acquired from missionary friends in his childhood, "Chris, we're moving into the age of the globally indigenous church. The United States has certain assets, experiences, and resources, but so do the African churches. Combined as one church, we will accomplish so much together." The African AG had now outgrown the US AG by five to one through the early 2000s. It was a church of prayer, faith, and power evangelism. The laborers from the African churches were many.

A few years before, sharing a meal with one of our US AG World Missions leaders serving in the Muslim context, I mentioned this burgeoning missions force from the sub-Saharan area. His response saddened me. After I asked this Caucasian American friend his thoughts about African American believers joining missional church planting teams in Africa's north, he remarked, "It won't work, Chris. Arab Muslim racism is too intense. They'll never accept the gospel from sub-Saharans." I was stunned and somewhat offended at the words—not at the fact of racism in North Africa but at how flatly definitive this leader was concluding, "It'll never work." Case closed. No effort will be expended in that direction.

While accurate about the racism, this unflinching position on the matter disheartened me. The Greeks and other Gentiles hated the Jews, but Paul and other Jewish believers, under Holy Spirit power and sheer obedience, planted the gospel among them anyway. They even convinced them through the gospel to be the body of Jesus together *with Jews*. How could we not plan for, believe for, and act in the same way in the face of racial hatred by lost people in the twenty-first century?

A year or so later, I shared this AGWM leader's expressed reticence with Lazarus. In all gentleness and with tears in his eyes, he asked a penetrating question, "Chris, why are your kids worthy of martyrdom and mine are not?"

Oh, man.

Then, in early 2013, Egypt's AG Superintendent and his son were traveling with me to Nairobi for the biennial AAGA meetings. This followed just a few short months after a divine appointment–type meeting of the Egyptian AG leaders and Pastor Lazarus, the leader of AG Africa, at a Cincinnati Panera in the midst of a windstorm that blew out power for over two million people as we met. (Yes, that happened while we broke bread together! "An unhappy prince of the power of the air?" asked Lazarus, making a reference to a moniker of the enemy found in Ephesians 2:2.) For the first time as far as we know, Arab North African AG leaders and sub-Saharan African AG leaders would be worshiping together and strategizing missions as one united team. To me, this was a very big deal in light of the vision and strategy of Ephesians 2 and 3 (laid out in the theology portion of this book) and the remaining task of Matthew 24:14.

Eleventh-hour harvesters were about to join together—Arab and sub-Saharan alike.

Chapter 30

CHANGE OF PLANS

Lazarus invited the Egypt AG Leadership team and me to join him in East Africa for the March 2013 biennial meeting of the Africa Assemblies of God Alliance. This would be the first time for any North African delegation to attend the AAGA meetings. My involvement was possible because of a decades-long special friendship with Sameh Sadik, who had also attended Regent University for his graduate studies. Sameh's father was now the AG Egypt superintendent (bishop), and all our paths had merged the year before in that Cincinnati Panera during a windstorm. From then until now, Lazarus had been creating the ingrafting moment for these key Arab church leaders into the rest of the Africa AG Alliance.

When the Sadiks and I arrived at the venue in Nairobi, we learned that Lazarus had left the conference early and returned home unexpectedly to Malawi. His mother had passed.

Oh no! Not only were we grieving for Lazarus, but we would miss him because he was chairing the AAGA meetings and was supposed to introduce the Egyptian delegation and vision cast the significance.

Now we knew no one at the meetings . . .

. . . until lunchtime the first day when in walked a longtime friend, Ron Swai! Just a handful of years earlier God had heart-level connected me with Ron as well.

Ron had been in a two-year graduate program with AGTS (Assemblies of God Theological Seminary), and we had shared a meal together at an

Africa's Hope meeting in the mid-2000s. When I learned that night that Ron wouldn't see his young family for two years—"Brother Chris, it's expensive to fly home for an East African. The Lord is faithful; we will be fine"—I just knew our church would want to do something about that. The Spirit began to knit us together for life.

On hearing about this back home, our church family couldn't even contemplate a parent not seeing his children for two years during their elementary years. Yet this was the kind of sacrifice this brother and his family were enduring to enhance his preparation for Kingdom leadership back home in Tanzania!

"Ron, could you visit our church over Thanksgiving break and greet the congregation?" I wanted to let the church meet this humble brother and understand the commitment and sacrifice he and his family were willing to walk in for the sake of the Kingdom. I just knew our body would give generously to send him home for Christmas. And they did.

That initial interlinking of our lives led later to missions partnering in Tanzania between our local church and the Bible school he led in the city of Mwanza. Our friendship grew.

Now, in early 2013, I was in Nairobi with the Egypt delegation with no Lazarus, alone in the Brackenhurst cafeteria, and in walked my dear friend Ron Swai with the Tanzania delegation to AAGA!

My eyes filled with tears as we embraced. Family was here to help us convey why the Sadiks had come. They wanted to join AAGA and invite us to co-labor for the harvest among unreached people groups on the continent and, in particular, Muslims in the north.

Ron wanted us to meet his superintendent, a gentle giant of a man with a disarming smile and a gentle, rolling, deep-chested laugh. His name was Barnabas. In just a few years, Barnabas would be the new president of AAGA and would quickly rise in servant leadership globally for the AG. Lazarus had opened the door. What was nonexistent before—north-south inclusive, multinational missions teams—would now begin to be dreamed and encouraged. An anointing from heaven was being poured onto all of it.

North Africa and sub-Saharan Africa leaders were now connected. When the Sadiks addressed the assembly of AAGA that March, the house erupted in cheers, worship, and celebration of the King of kings and this strategic conciliation of African hearts. The gates of hell were trembling.

God was up to something way bigger than we could have possibly planned or imagined, even if we had spent years trying.

Chapter 31

RACIALLY RECONCILING, ETHNICALLY INCLUSIVE, DIVERSELY UNITED

In every category that mattered to our hearts, from within our own local church to our city and to the nations, the Father was showing us in striking ways that *His heart* is for His whole church proclaiming, living, loving, and doing His whole gospel *together* in neighborhoods, counties, cities, and nations, across the earth.

Making disciples of all peoples, ministering in healing ways directly into the deepest societal fractures, and reaching the disbelieving lost with His truth, while tangibly righting societal wrongs through His Name and through Christ in us, is what He desires His church, including specific local churches, to be all about. That's the gospel.

To *know* you are in the truth, according to 1 John 3:23, is to believe in Christ *and* to love. You cannot have one without the other and still be a biblical Christian. As a church, we were beginning to more fully realize these principles of the Kingdom, and that they are both micro and macro, local and global, personal and societal. "Thy will be done on earth, as it is in heaven" (Matthew 6:10 KJV)—in literal expressions!

Then in the summer of 2013, the seeming racial status quo in America exploded. Cities were burning. From Ferguson to Baltimore, race relations were raw. And not enough people understood why. Glaringly, not enough people in the church of Jesus Christ understood why.

Chapter 32

IRRATIONAL RACIAL FEAR

As I've learned over the years from life-friends of color, black people simply don't live in the same America as the rest of us lighter-hued folk. If we have any level of calling to be reconcilers, and if we're in Christ, by definition we have this calling (2 Corinthians 5), and we must *know* this.

Two Americas exist.

To live black in America is to be made aware every day of your skin, your hair, your existence as an "other"—an "other" to be subconsciously feared and often, even more subconsciously, disdained.

In a meeting of Cincinnati evangelical and gospel-centered leaders on race, I once watched my friend Ray McMillian ask a prominent older evangelical of the lighter hue how often he thinks about his whiteness. Blinking at Pastor Ray for a moment, Dr. Jerry Kirk finally responded, "Never."

Then turning to special guest Dr. John M. Perkins, Ray reversed the question: "How often do you think of your blackness?" With zero hesitation, Dr. Perkins let the words "every day" fly from his mouth. Much of the room, full of more whites than blacks, sat wide-eyed and stunned.

Many whites just don't know this.

We don't know that our sisters and brothers suffer indignities every day. Could you imagine the sheer mental exhaustion from not knowing at any given cross-racial encounter whether you have to brace for foolishness, no matter how unintentional, subconscious, or misguided the occurrence may be? Exhausting. Degrading. Dehumanizing. That's living black in America.

Whites and blacks don't live in the same America.

And that only gets at the actual daily, interpersonal experiences, not to mention the exhaustion of living with the repercussions of decades and generations of negative inertia against your people group: From chattel slavery, the worst ever seen under heaven, to red lining to disproportionate policing, prosecuting, convicting, and sentencing for the very same crimes and mistakes as whites have committed! Look it all up. It won't take you long. Go ahead, Google it. Any one part of it. Read, educate yourself, turn off entertainment cable news and egregious talk radio and study the matter for real.

During the summer of 2013, it all just boiled over. I will give my best effort to explain why it boiled over in Cleveland, Baltimore, Ferguson, St. Paul, South Carolina, New York City, Baton Rouge, Dayton. Good grief! No, just grief.

Did black lives have any worth at all in this country?

Family after family decimated. The Father must have been weeping at our sin.

That summer so many unarmed young black men and boys died at the hands of police tasked with the job of protecting them, not killing them. And by no count whatsoever was it equal with whites being killed at the hands of fearful, over-reactive policing. Research the data.

Then, in Dallas that same summer, came an unconscionable mass execution of police officers by a former military young black man who had just had enough. Sinful, tragic, horrific. Our officers of the law should always be respected and feel supported, not targeted. As should young black men, who are also our sons.

What in the world was going on? What in America was going on?

Irrational racial fear.

And racism.

But the irrational racial fear of officers was killing young black men. Either that or officers subconsciously believed it was also their job to be judge, jury, and executioner. I don't believe that. Violent reaction of some in the black community was now placing innocent officers and their precious families in jeopardy.

Police brutality was a race control mechanism during Jim Crow and slavery—police brutality applied on purpose against African-descent people.

It was used to enforce racism in the deep South, from where most people of color in the rest of America had migrated in the 1910s and 1920s looking for a less oppressive life and for work. No wonder, with this historical reality between African Americans and police and with continuing disproportionate racialization of policing across America (more than you might realize), black folk across the country don't trust the police. By disproportionate racialization of policing, I mean how, nationally, black men are arrested, prosecuted, and jailed at a rate of six to one more than white men for the same crimes.

On the Thursday after the St. Paul, Minnesota, killing of Philando Castile broadcast live on Facebook, a handful of Cincinnati pastors issued a press release: At the first of the next week, Cincinnati faith leaders would release a statement on the status of police brutality in the land. Something needed to be said about the irrational racial fear clouding the judgment of good and bad officers alike.

Before the press conference could even take place, the Dallas officers were dead.

We were stunned and heartbroken by such a horrific week of death in our nation between young black men and the police. We held the press conference. Black and white pastors standing together in the name of Jesus, welcoming Jewish and Islamic leaders alongside as well, we declared this fear needed to stop. Too many brown and black men, and now police officers too, were losing their lives.

There was so much work to do.

Chapter 33

2014

This year would blow my mind. Four fascinating things happened.

1. Major national news outlets took an interest in multiracial, multi-ethnic, multi-economic church in America, including Peoples Church Cincinnati.
2. International missions was about to get crazy good with multiracial, multi-ethnic, multi-economic church and Great Commission efforts, at least within my own tribe, the Assemblies of God network. The Beyond Conference at Brackenhurst in Nairobi, Kenya, led by Dick and Jennifer Brogden and our AG World Missions senior team, was the inauguration.
3. The southern hemisphere church was a mostly sleeping potential global missions giant about to become more fully awake to their part in world evangelization.
4. A diversely united leadership of the Church of God in Christ and the AG were soon to declare together the worth of black lives in the midst of a season where the national validation of their worth was in question.

It turns out that the May 2012 *Los Angeles Times* story that included us, just weeks after our name change, was only initial evidence of the prophetic January 2012 *Cincinnati Enquirer* headline, "Christ Covets National Stage."

Not far into 2014 came a phone interview with Laura Meckler of the *Wall Street Journal*. Yes, that *Wall Street Journal*.

She wasn't talking just to Peoples Church Cincinnati. She was research-
ing this quickly growing phenomenon of churches moving from mono- to
multi-ethnic, multi-economic expression all across America. She'd first
noticed it during a visit to a Columbus, Ohio, church during her cov-
erage of the 2008 election as she was tasked with campaign reporting
on Republican presidential candidate John McCain. Her interest in this
church movement was piqued with what she witnessed that day. She
had long hoped to come back and find out what was going on with this.
Along the way, pastor friends leading incredible examples of Revelation
5:9 churches across the denominational and nondenominational landscape
had pointed her to us.

After we talked on the phone for about a half hour, she asked if she could
schedule a visit to talk to more people in the congregation. That late spring
or early summer, she flew into Cincy and spent Friday through Sunday visiting, listening, and probing into different groups and individuals at Peoples
Church, asking what this multiethnic, multieconomic church "phenomenon" was all about. It just seemed so remarkable to her.

I remember at the end of her time, after a particularly exciting Starbucks
coffee shop discussion with young professional singles in the church, she
asked about sending a videographer for another weekend.

Little did we realize what an extensive, deep dive she was taking into the
multiethnic church movement, or how our midsize, Midwest expression
of it was to be helpful to her for a closer look beyond the research and
national interviews. It was just so much fun to show the world what God
was doing! We prayed that the evidence of His purchase on the Cross—a
people for Himself of every tribe, language, and nation, albeit imperfect and
still working it out—would demand a verdict about Jesus from those who
read her story. A verdict of "yes"—a verdict of belief in Him.

That same summer, I met with a friend who was slipping from the
faith despite our hours of earnest discussion together. He was the son of a
prominent, national evangelical leader. Before moving to another state, he
wanted to give me his famous father's monogrammed Bible. As we stood in
our church parking lot, he pointed over his shoulder and offered, "If what's
happening here goes national, that would cause me to believe again." How
biblical.

"Father, unite them as you and I are united. Not only these eleven, but also those who will believe after them. Unite them in such a way that the world will believe you sent me" (John 17:20-23, my paraphrase).

Later that fall, 2014, Laura Meckler's groundbreaking WSJ story headline was centered onto the front page with a full-spread article that followed inside the first section of the paper. But that wasn't the only thing of prophetic note going on in 2014. God was also pressing out His aspects of His *worldwide* vision for the church-like-heaven-on-earth.

Just a few years earlier, Dick and Jennifer Brogden had welcomed Jan and me into their flat in Cairo, Egypt. It was actually a two-flat space: one for life and one for training multinational teams to LiveDead (a "take up your cross and follow me" missions strategy of diverse teams planting churches) among unreached people groups—distinct socio-ethnic and language groups without a church planting movement among them and less than 1 percent believers.

Already for a decade we had dreamed and discussed together, Beards and Brogdens, the idea of every tribe, language, and people involved in missional teams living and planting the gospel among UPGs. How compelling, how effective, how biblical would this be!

Now in 2014, the vision along with UPG emphasis was being cast across the entire US AGWM leadership. Only one thing was missing: all the rest of the AG missional folk from the other two hundred or more nations.

Well, there was a sprinkling of them. Some from sub-Saharan Africa, and some from Latin America, Europe, and Central Asia. That was good. That was a beginning. Things of the Kingdom of God often start as the smallest of seeds.

There was a spiritual detonation taking place in Nairobi that week. Global missions as heaven on earth was about to catch fire in a radically new way.

Chapter 34

TANZANIA

In early 2014, in the Lord's providence and timing, Jan and I were sent by Peoples Church Cincinnati from the Nairobi "Beyond Conference" to Tanzania. We had been invited by Barnabas Mtokambali to the city of Mbeya for teaching a theology of missions at a gathering of a hundred TAG (Tanzania Assemblies of God) senior leaders.

After a brief stop first in Ethiopia and a beautiful visit to see friends and family of our congregation, we arrived in the lush green highland area of Mbeya, Tanzania. There we spent a week of friendship as well as delving into the essence of and some praxis relevant to Matthew 24:14. "This gospel of the kingdom will be preached in the whole world as a testimony to all nations [*ethnos*], and then the end will come."

Tanzania AG was working through a captivating ten-year vision and strategic plan. In these years they would grow from 2,800 pastors to 10,000, from 2,300 churches to 10,000, and from 600,000 members to 3 million, in a country with about 45 million in population. Now, five years into the work that began in 2009, they were on schedule. Noticeably small to me at that time in their strategic plan, however, was their missionary number. They would add ten over ten years. What if for the next ten-year strategic plan through 2030 they included 1,000 missionaries, a tithe of the 10,000 pastors? Easy for me to say, but it was truly burning in my heart to humbly share this with them.

With that question on my heart, I asked Barnabas his blessing to teach with all my being the implications of Matthew 24:14 for all the church, including the Tanzanian AG.

Jesus said, "This gospel of the kingdom will be preached in the whole world as a testimony to all nations, and then the end will come" (Matthew 24:14, italics mine). For this task to ever be completed in the earth, it would require the whole church taking the whole gospel into all the world together, to every people.

From the Joshua Project (JoshuaProject.net) list, we knew the world had about seven thousand people groups, distinct sociolinguistic people groups without a substantial witness of the gospel of Jesus Christ or any known reproducing churches among them.

Within the global missiology, vision, and philosophy of my own church network, the U.S. Assemblies of God, I wondered if we had substantively included the vision that newly reached groups and nations should not only be self-governing, self-supporting, and self-propagating but also self-missionizing and self-theologizing, leaning wholeheartedly into the work of Matthew 24:14 with the rest of the global church.

One of the fruits we were experiencing at Peoples Church Cincinnati was that every voice, every gift, every perspective, every people group in the church proves an essential contributor to the work of ministry in our body, in our city, and on our missions teams. Why not also throughout the global church in full engagement with Jesus' global mission?

Our body and board back home were praying for us and for our work on this three-part trip. I'll always remember how one of our deacons called me on our way to Tanzania. "Chris, I think on our behalf, and on behalf of our US AG churches who sent missionaries to Tanzania seventy-five years ago, you should ask forgiveness—forgiveness for not having fully explained and encouraged Great Commission work to the nations as an essential and nonnegotiable part of the work of the Kingdom for them to do, in the same way as it is for us." I remember immediately knowing this was the Lord, but also realizing I could only do this as an act of identificational repentance, like Daniel repenting for the sins of his fathers, and in no official capacity. But yes, this insight resonated profoundly in my soul as from the Lord.

For five days I shared biblical vision and theology for missional thought, basic missiological information, missions prioritizing, along with praxis and action for every believer, every church, every part of the body in all the earth. At the end of the week, I shared what our deacon had called me to say, and then I did what that word guided me to do. After I asked their forgiveness for a shortsighted effort and incomplete understanding of indigenous missions principles exercised by us in prior decades, Barnabas responded before his group of General Presbyters (regional overseers) and national department leaders. Looking me in the eye, he expressed this: "This apology deserves a response. And we will give it. We forgive you. And thank you for this." Then looking toward his leadership team seated in the room before him, he added, "Friends, we've had the Bible in our language for seventy-five years, and there is no excuse. What our brother and the Word of God has challenged us to do, we will do with all our hearts in the years ahead."

Jan and I were stunned. We had so many takeaways that week from Pastor Barnabas and the TAG. Our hearts were on fire from observing their fasting and prayer, strategic planning processes, and passionate action to make disciples and plant many churches across all of Tanzania. "Tanzania for Jesus" was more than a slogan for them; it was happening, and at an almost unimaginably rapid rate.

Barnabas provided me a translated ten-page summary of the ten-year plan and shared the story of how they used a prayerful consensus process to arrive at this plan they were now working with all their hearts.

I could only imagine what it could mean if this model of prayer, passion, planning, and action were contextually adopted and executed in the United States and across the earth, especially for the evangelization of every tribe, language, nation, and people. How amazing it would be to see Christ bring healing to brokenness in societies through transformed people and the collective, smart social engagement of the resulting growing and multiplying churches.

One thing for sure was clear: The AG network in the earth was on the verge of big change. Good change. God-ordained change. And the catalyzing would come because of the manifold wisdom emanating from diverse Kingdom unity guided by multiethnic leadership teams under Christ. Church-like-heaven-on-earth. Ephesians 3:9-10.

The year 2014 was a year of propulsion.

Chapter 35

BLACK LIVES DO MATTER

In December 2014, Dr. George O. Wood had declared the Assemblies of God (AG) would join the Church of God In Christ's (COGIC) appeal for a Sunday validating the truth that black lives have worth in the face of the flood of lives lost at the hands of police when no gun was present.

It would be called Black Lives Matter Sunday.

I tweeted, "Peoples Church is in!"

A few moments later a COGIC pastor friend of mine, Rev. Michael McBride, texted from Berkley, California, to see if I was willing to be interviewed about this joint COGIC/AG expression. I thought he meant for his church blog or Sunday service, and I agreed.

Then my phone rang from an Atlanta number. I let it go to voicemail. I hadn't realized it was CNN! Could I call back and confirm to interview on national news with Michael on Black Lives Matter Sunday?

Yes, yes I could!

What a strategic and precious opportunity this would be to display a loving relationship in the church between black and white servant leaders and demonstrate how heart-level friendship and facing matters head-on together is the way out of irrational racial fear, racism, and enmity.

That Sunday, we went on live TV together.

Racial reconciliation often deepens when diverse friends stand as friends when it really matters most. This was that kind of moment.

That Monday, I feared Dr. Wood would be coming under fire by his own constituency. Racial ignorance and political fear is so high concerning matters of race that often white Christians completely miss the real pain being suffered by real people—by our church family members of color. To say that black lives have worth—when day after day that year societal messaging and events seemed to be shouting otherwise—was very bold and could be misunderstood by many.

It was.

Godly leadership sets its jaw like a flint anyway and leads the way forward into the principles of the Kingdom, regardless of how well the team yet understands.

Understanding will come. The price of backlash by those not yet comprehending does exact a toll. But it's worth every bit of pain if we love them and love those refreshed by the yet little understood, principled, reconciliatory stands we humbly take in matters of race. The key is to teach, model, and teach again, showing from Scripture and facts the power of what we are doing.

Chapter 36

RACIALLY RECONCILING CHURCHES AND AMERICAN CITIES

As the years progressed, we were seeing the possibilities of Ephesians 3:9-10. What a joy to watch the kaleidoscopic richness of the Lord's splendor lived out in the earth and announced into the heavenlies, as discussed in Part 1 of this book.

Many people were coming to Christ, and Peoples Church Cincinnati was growing. We were also planting new churches under diverse leadership.

We were also experiencing the Lord leading us, with diverse others, into developing interdenominational ties along with working with gospel-rooted organizations in our city for racial and biblical justice. We did every endeavor in the name of our Savior, Jesus, for His name, for His renown, and for the influence of His ways among us. The words of Isaiah 26:8 pulsed in our hearts: "Your name and renown are the desire of our hearts."

As our congregation grew interracially and interethnically—going deeper through small groups, corporate worship, and times of family celebration— our life stories, our cultures, and our histories began to immensely enrich one another's lives.

So by the mid-2010s, not only were we experiencing that manifold wisdom and richness among us spiritually (Ephesians 3:10), but we were also developing reconciling and biblical justice hearts for the matters affecting our church family members' lives.

This meant that peace with our families of origin and personal, partisan political ideas took a back seat to our Kingdom unitedness (see Matthew 12:48-50). This happened without any compromise of biblical and gospel principles; in fact, in many respects their amplification, was taking place. To be pro-life now meant so much more than preborn babies but absolutely still included them.

We were also thinking and strategizing in a pro-life way about the babies *after* they were born. What was the family structure circumstance, and why? What was the family economic situation, and why? What could be done immediately?

Someone has said compassion is to care, but when we start asking the "why" questions we start to think about biblical justice. Isaiah 58–61, Jesus' ministry manual, had become dear to us. We were now more than ever looking for ways to live it out. (Please take the time to read Isaiah 58 through 61 right now, before moving on.)

In the late summer of 2014, Ferguson, Missouri, erupted. Then, we heard of one after another of police-involved shootings or deaths of African American human beings. It seemed surreal. This was affecting our church family deeply. We were white, brown, and black, and what affected one affected all. And this seeming "open season" on black lives by the evil one was horrific to us.

By now we had learned that racial reconciliation was much deeper than *kumbaya*.

Up till now, the American church had held many foot-washing and reconciliation services. Until we begin to feel one another's pain and move to relieve it together (bearing one another's burdens), however, we won't experience truly authentic reconciling relationships.

Before, when our church was homogeneous white, we simply didn't feel the pain of others different from us, and we didn't really care that much. Things were different now in 2014. St. Louis had burned, Cleveland was in an uproar, Baltimore was about to blow, and St. Paul was a tinderbox. An unarmed African American man running in fear after a bizarre police interaction in South Carolina was shot to death in his back. This was heinous and inconceivable! Yet it seemed to keep happening week after week.

In Cincinnati, we had our own tragic police-involved cross-racial shooting death, and it took place just blocks from our church campus. Unarmed Sam DuBose was shot point-blank in the head by officer Ray Tensing after being pulled over for missing a front license plate. How many years had I driven without a front license plate and was never pulled over? Decades.

We could ask what would happen if people acted differently when pulled over, but that would disregard the historic distrust and abject fear on the part of African Americans for the police—and for legitimate reasons. And that's not to say that police don't have fears, but this is what they heroically sign up for: to put themselves in harm's way to serve and protect all lives. All lives matter equally.

Until they don't.

We had only learned the plentiful data and anecdotal evidence from one another and through research as we became one church—black, white, and brown—loving Jesus and one another.

Sam DuBose, a father of nine, was shot dead just blocks from our church campus. What would happen now? In the summer of 2015, Cincinnati was about to find out.

Chapter 37

UNIVERSITY OF CINCINNATI, PEOPLES CHURCH, AND CORINTHIAN BAPTIST

The news broke. An unarmed father of nine was shot in the head by a young University of Cincinnati (UC) police officer after a traffic stop for a license plate infraction went horrifically bad.

Just months before Sam DuBose's shooting death, UC President Santa Ono and I had shared a serendipitous visit together at his office.

UC is located just blocks from our church campus. I had learned of President Ono's faith in Jesus Christ through a friend. It was through a ministry called InterVarsity that he'd come to faith. I reached out to him as a pastor and a local church/community leader. I simply wanted to develop rapport and let him know I was in his corner and loving his leadership of our university, which was flourishing under his direction.

Little did I realize how important our new relational tie would prove to be when police brutality against people of color by one of the university officers visited our Uptown Cincinnati neighborhood.

For some time, I had been hearing from immigrant members of our church that UC police were aggressive and disrespectful, even toward nuclear families just walking near campus together. This concerned me deeply, but never did I think another flagrant police shooting would take place. Not in our town. After all, we had in place a community and police Collaborative Agreement (CA) that had markedly changed police-community relations in Cincinnati. That was before I learned that the CA was only with the Cincinnati Police Department, not any other Cincinnati area municipality departments, and not with UC police.

Hours after Sam's shooting death, my friend Rev. KZ Smith reached out and invited me to a meeting at his church campus, also in Uptown near UC.

I remember entering the room filled with African American friends, clergy, and community leaders, as well as Dr. Santa Ono and a team of six or seven leaders from the university, including the UCPD chief, and UC's general counsel (lead lawyer).

I felt palpable tension in the room. Sam's death was just hours old. Everyone wondered what would happen now.

KZ and I had shared friendship for nearly twenty years at this point. His heart for Christ, easy smile, wise leadership, and the trust he'd earned from the people and leaders of our city were always such attractive traits about him. We had shared meals, ministry, and press conferences. We trust each other. We love each other. We both had grown up in our city; we both had shared our personal histories with each other. We are friends.

As I sat next to KZ who was chairing the meeting, I also looked across the table and deep into President Santa Ono's eyes. His face revealed the concern and grief that gripped him.

We were gathered to work through the situation. We were gathered in respect, but also without media. KZ had required they stay in the parking lot. Dozens of them were there—poised journalists, news vans, and cameras.

This intense meeting was for connecting in earnest and working through this awful tragedy with deep change in view. Two families were totally wrecked, DuBose's and Tensing's. And African American leaders in the room wanted answers and action. What was UC going to do? How could this even happen? What was going on with the UC police department? Why were they policing so far off campus, blocks away in neighborhoods of color?

Suddenly, KZ leaned over and quietly told me he had just been notified of a hospital emergency (one of his church members was dying). He needed me to facilitate the meeting. Oh, and by the way, the attorney general's office was sending a couple of officials to our meeting, and they would arrive any minute. Then he slipped out of the room. To this day I haven't remembered to ask him what happened. To step out in crucial moments is not like him; he's ice under fire. He's also a quintessential shepherd pastor.

But now I was leading alone. Yet not alone and not really leading, just facilitating. The group of leaders in the room facing UC leadership loved and trusted each other. We were a team leaning into a profoundly dangerous moment for our city.

Over the next hour or two, the collective team worked through key issues.

» The officer was fired.
» The university would provide scholarships for all nine of Sam's children.
» The university was filled with remorse.
» The university police department would withdraw from surrounding neighborhoods to on-campus policing only.
» The UCPD would have total leadership changes.
» The UCPD would undergo an analysis of all their policing practices, and there would be a new community accountability committee.
» UCPD would join the Collaborative Agreement.

Throughout the meeting, key community leaders—like Iris Roley, a signal architect of the 2003 Collaborative Agreement, and my clergy friends of color—wisely and profoundly led a process that UC was willing to join, working their way through the many meaningful decisions.

At times, trust was so low between the university and community that we weren't sure matters could be resolved, but all at the table were sincere.

Then suddenly the Justice Department officials arrived. They barged into the private meeting and, holding the door open while glancing around the large boardroom-style table, asked who was in charge. Well, I wasn't really in charge, but I was facilitating per Pastor KZ's request, so I inquired, "Who is asking?"

Looking at me, the officer sternly shot back, "And who are you?"

I gave my name and church, and then asked if we could chat in the hallway. The two officials looked at each other and back at me. I quickly added, "We're in a very crucial private meeting here between the parties involved and their representatives. Can I meet you in the hallway to understand your purpose here today?" I really didn't understand at all and was very concerned about the delicate trust and forward momentum of the meeting being derailed.

In the hallway, the officer first gave a bad joke while showing me his credentials, not cracking a smile, "I'm here to arrest everyone in there." I just stared at him. That frustrated me. Inside I was asking the Holy Spirit for help and wisdom. Then the officer smiled and said, "No, we're here to convey a message and enlist help. We have intel that agitators are coming to Cincinnati tonight, and we need the help of that room to quell any potential violence."

I responded, "Sir, what's happening in that room is something we need happening in cities all across the country. May I suggest you say what you need to say quickly and then observe the careful work going on in there?" My heart was racing. The female official smiled with warmth and understanding and agreed to my request. We reentered the room.

Looking around the table, the DOJ officer explained, "We have reason to believe things in the city could become violent tonight. We need the help of the clergy in this room. And we're asking you to be among the young people helping to keep order."

One of the seasoned pastors of color spoke up. "Look, what will keep the peace in this city tonight is what is accomplished in this room. We have no control whatsoever over the grief and anger our young people are experiencing, but this meeting can help. I suggest you let us get back to work."

Seemingly stunned by our united resolve, the officials thanked everyone for their time and stayed a while to observe the proceedings before quietly slipping out and going on their way. We never heard from them again.

After the meeting I texted Santa Ono.

"Thank you for your leadership, your humility, your intensity to do what is needed," I typed out. He asked me what else he could do. Simply, I responded, "Do what you say you will do." He did. UC did. And that night, unlike in April 2001, the city did not burn.

In the end, the officer was charged with murder.

Racial peace and reconciliation require justice. Justice simply means making wrong things right. No one can bring a dead father or son back to life, but clear wrongs must be made right. President Ono did what he could do to the best of his ability. Our city is better for it.

But we still have much work to do.

THE HARD WORK OF RACIAL RECONCILIATION INCLUDES RACIAL JUSTICE

THE WORK AT THE UNIVERSITY OF CINCINNATI

In 2015, the University of Cincinnati went through a change of presidents. Santa Ono took leadership of Canadian University in Vancouver, which is larger than UC and a university he grew up around because his own father taught there.

After Sam DuBose's death, a Police Community Accountability program was solidly in place with key clergy and community leaders involved. I personally opted to join the President's Diversity Council as a community rep and assist in the racial inclusion future of UC in faculty, staff, and student levels. The percentages of African Americans at all levels of UC in 2015 were not good. For a university located in an urban environment of a metropolitan American city, this was inexcusable.

Would the new president embrace the diversity council's work? Time would tell. But he did. President Pinto came with similar passion and palpable resolve to harness the university's diversity potential, especially the inclusion of at-risk populations like Cincinnati's African American community. How fantastic! The entire team of educators and administrators under Bleuzette Marshall's adept leadership and President Pinto's attentive, intense involvement promises a bright future for diverse inclusion at UC. Cincinnati will be better for it.

THE WORK IN THE CITY

At-risk schools

For racial and biblical justice and equity to occur in our city, something has to be done about urban education. Over the years, local ministries and organizations have recognized this and have stepped in to help. In the 2000s, Cincinnati's City Gospel Mission jumped in with a student mentoring and tutoring program called Whiz Kids. Churches and teams of Christ followers began coming alongside to "adopt" specific urban neighborhood schools.

Multiethnic and multieconomic churches have stepped into serving schools. These churches seem uniquely aware and leveraged to make an impact due to cross-racial relationship, cross-economic strength, and cross-cultural awareness not usually found in homogenous church congregations, no matter how much they care.

One prime example is Bethel Cincinnati, a gospel-centered diverse church that has led the way to tackle the challenges at Rockdale Elementary in Avondale, one of our city's historically segregated, black neighborhoods. With 80 percent of the Rockdale kids on free and reduced lunch, with Cincinnati owning a top-five worst child poverty rate among major American cities, and with our city public schools being majority African American children with 70 percent of students from single-parent households, CPS cannot by itself make up for the many decades of generational, racially concentrated poverty and fatherlessness. Churches and community partners getting involved is essential.

Similar to what Peoples Church has done at Taft Elementary, new multiracial and multi-economic churches in Cincinnati have been stepping into the need. In each case, within a few years, schools have experienced substantial turnaround, meaning measurable improvements in the prospects of the children attending there.

But our city's number three standing in the nation child poverty rating won't be turned around by great tutors. Economics for families will have to change. Children are poor because parents are poor.

Second-chance hiring

We are learning through our multiracial, multi-economic church life that many people coming to Christ out of broken and poor backgrounds are returning citizens or people with felony records whom employers won't hire. If you can't work, you can't provide. If you can't provide, you and your family will be poor. Children raised in the constant stress of racially concentrated poverty become captive to generational poverty. These children often live in single-parent households.

We have also found that this ex-offender, second-class-citizen-for-life reality is being lived out in a racially disproportionate way in Cincinnati. We have found that for the same crimes, black youth go to jail eight times more than white youth. For decades and with devastating generational effects. Someone needs to start talking about this. Why not multiracial, multi-economic churches? So we're talking, but we're also taking action in prayer and direct engagement.

In addition to putting these facts of racial disproportionality in the light for the church of Cincinnati and for the community at large, we also have been working on solutions through a second-chance hiring initiative and through applying corporate prayer to these matters. If employers can be protected from the threat of negligent hiring lawsuits (a fear more than a reality, but nonetheless a felt fear), then just maybe they will hire second-chance folk, especially when labor markets are tight. And during the last few years of President Obama's administration, the labor market was tightening.

I remember meeting Dan Meyer for the first time. I'd learned about him through the paper. He was an entrepreneur with heart, a Catholic Christ follower who had started a manufacturing company to profit with purpose. When I met him, he'd already hired about forty people with criminal records and had employed a social worker with a vision to walk alongside these folks, and he was seeing a lower employee turnover rate than ever previously in his thirty-five years of manufacturing experience.

For each person employed, he and his business partner, Richard Palmer, were seeing ten lives economically enhanced. In only seven years, their company, Nehemiah Manufacturing, was doing $50 million annually.

Over lunch, we shared our mutual vision for a business alliance of such companies. Employers who would have a "give back" heart but who would also benefit from this outstanding discovery: People given a second chance tend to be unusually loyal and hard-working employees.

Oh, we had challenges to overcome. Soft skills had to be learned, along with transportation and housing issues to be solved, especially in the first few months of employment. But because of the deep and long-term positive effects, lives are being changed, families are holding together, and our city's poverty rates will ultimately be affected. Within a few years of our first lunch, the Beacon of Hope Business Alliance was formed, and what Nehemiah Manufacturing was learning could begin to scale.

At this writing, over seventy business partners enjoy the mission and successes of second-chance hiring. Nehemiah alone has over eighty second-chance employees.

Public policy work
Little did I understand how much evangelism alone would not accomplish. Obviously God understood this, too. Why else would he have such powerful admonitions to the people of God "to loose the chains of injustice" as found in Isaiah 58:6? And at the same time, to break chains but not introduce the King of kings would be spiritually empty.

What if we did both, offering both righteousness and justice, realizing that both of these Kingdom elements comprise His rulership as described in Psalm 89:14? "Righteousness and justice are the foundation of your throne; love and faithfulness go before you." Both justice and righteousness are the foundations of His throne, His rulership, His Kingdom.

With these principles at heart, along with talented believers from our gospel-centered Cincinnati congregations and other not-yet-believing marketplace friends, we went to work on specific societal injustices.

As mentioned earlier, in our city someone could be convicted for a crime for which others would not be (especially people of color over and above Caucasians). Even for those who served their time justly, if they were guilty, they could pay their debt to society and still *never* fully be "out of jail." The conviction on their record kept them unemployed, no matter how many job applications and résumés they submitted day after day, month after month. Employers were not hiring former felons. Period.

Something needed to be done. Preaching the gospel alone, or only praying, would not solve this conundrum. God's people would have to roll up their sleeves and do some prayerful, thoughtful public policy work.

How would we do this? Through strategic partnerships.

Chapter 39

DAVID SINGLETON

The first time I became aware of this man was seeing his picture on a 2006 cover of a local magazine, *City Beat*, and the brief description, "A Giant for Justice." His work and the work of his organization, the Ohio Justice and Policy Center (OJPC), revolved around helping ex-felons get back on their feet for life. David Singleton had my attention.

This Harvard lawyer, man of color, and brilliant, godly leader was giving his life and talents to change life for others who couldn't do that on their own. No matter how transformed through Christ their hearts might be, they couldn't get jobs. Discipleship of new believers such as these usually meets disruption around that fact. David and OJPC were chain breakers (Isaiah 58), removing barriers for people and allowing churches like ours to maintain forward momentum when discipling new ex-felon, Christ followers.

In 2011, OJPC worked steadfastly on legislation that would provide employer protection to hire rehabilitated ex-felons, a Certificate of Qualification for Employment (CQE). During an Ohio criminal justice senate committee hearing, fellow evangelical pastor Peterson Mingo and I shared testimony.

My story before the committee was about a young man in our church and how, with smart bipartisan public policy help, community leaders and churches like ours could help break poverty cycles. Pastor Mingo shared his story of coming to Christ and then making life work after serving years incarcerated for murder. Both Republicans and Democrats sat spellbound as this elder of color shared the public policy change help he needed for mentoring the young urban men he was mentoring in Cincinnati. Could we in Ohio pass smart new public policy that would allow them to work?

In the summer of 2012, Governor Kasich signed into law the Certificate of Qualification for Employment (CQE). The way it works is that an ex-offender stays clean for one year, completes a job readiness program, returns to his or her court of record, and applies for a CQE (which protects a prospective employer from negligent hiring lawsuits). Within a few short years, this brilliant, simple, common sense solution paved the way for the birth and growth of the Beacon of Hope Business Alliance. Without the expertise of OJPC and David Singleton's team, we'd have never gotten there. One of his staff colleagues, Stephen Johnson-Grove, personally crafted the legislation.

Breaking chains of injustice.

Why unjust chains? Because these people had already paid their debt to society for their crimes. They now needed the ability to work for a living, to stay out of prison, and to be fathers to their children and legal providers for their families. They had the opportunity now.

Chapter 40

THE WORK OF THE CHURCH OF CINCINNATI

Imagine in a city or county, one united body, many congregations, all under Christ, the whole church, ministering the whole gospel, in the whole city.

For sharing a story of the heterogeneous church in Cincinnati working as a collective, I want to take us back a couple of decades first.

Since the mid-1990s, the Holy Spirit had placed unifying, collective vision in Kingdom leaders' hearts in Cincinnati, and probably for many years prior as well. The first time I personally saw a written expression of these ideas was reading a book titled *Primary Purpose: Making It Hard for People to Go to Hell from Your City* by Pastor Ted Haggard. He captured what was stirring in many hearts at that time.

The premise: The church working cooperatively together in the name of Jesus ministering both proclamation and application of the whole gospel in a city could so "raise the water level of the Holy Spirit" there that churches would grow and multiply, believers would be on the increase, and the city's ills would be on the decrease. This vision was growing in my heart for Cincinnati and in the hearts of many other local leaders as well. In those years while Ted was healthy in his walk with Christ and serving with integrity (he later suffered some painful missteps), he was leading an astonishingly insightful vision. Colorado Springs was experiencing so much blessing. Even the pastors of color there shared that view with me once on a visit to the city.

So, over the years, while working on racial reconciliation and diverse inclusion through Christ in Peoples Church as a local body, we were also simultaneously working with other leaders on a collective vision for Greater Cincinnati as a whole.

During a 1998 June meeting of Kingdom leaders at our church campus with twenty-five pastors and leaders racially and denominationally diverse, we asked the question, "What would happen if we worked cooperatively and unselfishly under the name of Jesus for the evangelization and blessing of our city—the whole church, ministering the whole gospel, to the whole city?" After posing that question, where the flow of the meeting went next would change our lives and our city.

PART IV

Covenant Groups, Race to Unity, City Servants

Chapter 41

THE WHOLE CHURCH, THE WHOLE GOSPEL, THE WHOLE CITY

We didn't even yet understand the spiritual power and amplified practical influence of *diverse* unity, not theologically, anyway, and not experientially, yet. But we were intent on the question of what a united church of Jesus Christ could accomplish in a state, region, county, and city.

So we invited a gathering of busy leaders—young and old, black and white, clergy and parachurch, across the interdenominational spectrum—from gospel-centered, Bible-rooted ministries. Twenty-three of the twenty-five we had invited came. That alone demonstrated a keen interest in such a vision.

Dr. Jerry Kirk and Dr. Anderson Culbreath provided the necessary seasoned, godly experience to the meeting. These two men had served and led life-giving Kingdom change in our city for many years from two of Cincinnati's influential and trusted anchor churches.

I remember Jerry asking the question, "What is it you want to accomplish here?" A small group of younger leaders, composed of a microcosm of the diversity collected in the room, were catalyzing this particular meeting.

I remember speaking up. "Sir, we want to explore this question—what good things could happen in our city in the years ahead if the church of

Jesus Christ worked cooperatively in the spirit of mutual blessing to see the work of the gospel increase in our city?"

Almost immediately, KZ Smith spoke up. "Chris, if I get on this bus, I want to know where it's going. Ten years ago, I came to this church for a meeting supposedly like this, and we were all asked to get in a church van to go protesting together at an abortion clinic. People were getting arrested. Black people don't want to get arrested, Chris. I'm as pro-life as the rest of you here, but I need to know where this bus is going." We were just starting to get to know each other. Within time, I would more fully understand and appreciate what he was saying when he said, "Black people don't want to get arrested, Chris."

My response was to try again to articulate the vision that Galen Jones, Troy Jackson, Roger Howell, Erwin Goedicke, and I were working on. "KZ, what if we all worked as one heart, one mind, mutually blessing each other and together mutually blessing the city through Christ in us and Christ in our churches? Many people would come to salvation and broken things in our city would be made whole." The vision was powerful in my mind, but promised far too much in KZ's. I didn't really understand.

But then, Dwight Wilkins shared.

Dwight was pastoring a flourishing, Word-rooted, Spirit-embracing congregation in Avondale, one of our city's historic, black neighborhoods. The 1960s race riots had centered there. The community was now racially isolated, impoverished, and in need of new life. Wilkins was a bridge person, generationally, in that room. He was one of the youngest ever to lead the Baptist Ministers Conference of Cincinnati, in the mid-1980s, followed by KZ. They were close.

Dwight spoke up.

"Chris, we've been here before, after the Billy Graham mission and other such events in the 1970s and '80s. You all [white leaders] asked us to join the efforts, bring our people. We did. We asked in return that you all join us in improving our kids' schools, solving urban problems. You promised to, then you walked away after the evangelism events. Twice."

Dwight began to weep.

"Once after [a major citywide stadium evangelism event] in the early 1980s, we had a backyard barbecue together as clergy. We black leaders asked again when and how we might work on urban schools together. You all said, 'We can't do that. Our people wouldn't understand.' The event ended. We went our separate ways, and that was that."

Dwight began to sob, then heave and convulse with grief. The room was stunned and quiet. This hulking man of God, a former Ohio State defensive lineman under Woody Hays, was pouring out his heart. Two older white leaders nervously left the meeting. The rest of us sat spellbound, unsure what to do next. Then Jerry Kirk spoke, moving on as if Dwight had not even shared.

"Chris, what are you younger guys asking of us?" He didn't know how to acknowledge Dwight's pain.

I heard these words come from my mouth. "Sir, we'd like the baton. And we'd like to begin right here where Dwight is."

Anderson Culbreath spoke next. "Young men, if we're still right where we were twenty years ago, as far as I'm concerned, you can take it from here. I'm tired."

There was little else, and the meeting was over. People shuffled out.

Another bridge leader of color in the room, Michael Dantley, moved intently around the table to say privately, "Chris, if you guys are serious about starting where Dwight is, I'm in." That was a key God moment.

Something important was about to start. But we didn't know what or how.

That same day, after the meeting, I received a call from another younger white leader who had been seated next to Dwight. It was Jerry Kirk's successor at College Hill Presbyterian, Pat Hartsock. Pat's voice was excited and intense. "Chris, we need to start right where Dwight is as an end in itself. If we can't heal where he's hurting, we can't go forward!"

Immediately in my spirit I knew he was exactly right. We needed to see healing at our deepest church fracture in the city as an "end in itself" and not as a means to another end, no matter how Kingdom-centered the other goal might seem. Reconciliation was now the goal.

"What do we do next? How do we start?" Pat asked.

"Why don't you call Dwight since you've been meeting monthly for lunch already?" I urged. "I will call Michael Dantley," with whom I'd been meeting monthly for mentoring. "Let's ask them what we do next." Pat agreed.

And that's what we did.

Chapter 42

RACIAL MYTHS SHATTERED

Michael holds an EdD. Dwight was chaplain at University Hospital in Uptown.

They suggested we meet monthly over a meal in the physicians' lunchroom at what is now known as UC Medical Center, for friendship and sincere conversations about race, as brothers in Christ.

Pat and I needed our brothers to help us as act as "race physicians," mentors on matters of race. We had no idea how ignorant we really were about the black experience in America or how much our ignorance as white Christians contributes to the problems.

As an educator, Michael offered to walk us through societal racial myths and history and to help us together explore personal and heart-level discussions from those as our hinge points.

Our hearts were open. We were about to learn so much.

After just six meetings or so, our friendships were already going deep. We laughed, cried, and sat silently together at times. Our hearts were so full as we unpacked our stuff, grieved with one another, shared our stories, and heard much we'd never known.

At one point we asked the question: Shouldn't others in Cincinnati Christian leadership have the richness of this experience?

Together we identified about seven pairs of evangelical pastors and parachurch leaders we knew were already enjoying intentional cross-racial friendships. We invited them to a meeting to cast a vision.

Dwight chose a known soul food restaurant in one of Cincinnati's few racially mixed neighborhoods, College Hill. Most of our neighborhoods, as is the case in many American cities, are completely segregated. But in College Hill, the environment felt welcoming to all of us. There we spoke with fourteen leaders, mostly pastors, over griddled cornbread pancakes, candied yams, fried chicken, and hot sauce.

We asked if these men would join us in six months of relationally exploring and discussing racial myths, under Michael Dantley's leadership. All agreed. There was already an appetite in their hearts for what racial reconciliation in the church could mean for our city.

And racial healing in the church of Cincinnati was about to begin.

Within time, the city would never be the same. But first, there were rough waters ahead.

Chapter 43

RACE TO UNITY

At one of our racial myth meetings, Pastor Ray McMillian wanted to introduce a new topic: unchecked patriotism in white evangelicals.

We didn't like it. We complained to Michael and Dwight, and they allowed us to ask Ray to stop. In effect, we kicked him out of the group. Our shared lunch after the meeting that same day was a strange, hollow experience the cornbread pancakes didn't soothe.

For most of my life I had enjoyed the idea that my Founding Fathers were evangelical Christians. That my country was special, started almost by Jesus Himself. But I had never looked at all this through the eyes of my sisters and brothers of color. In what ways was America's beginning godly from their view? In what ways could the mostly racist founding fathers of the nation be heroes for them? Little did we realize how powerful a divide this was, complicating unity in the American church. Complicating unity in the church of Cincinnati.

Looking back, it makes total sense to me now, but at the time, we were frustrated. How could we racially reconcile if some believers felt we were tearing away at their identity, or what they thought was their identity . . . until we landed on our identity in Jesus Christ. Thanks to Ray, we got there. But it wasn't easy.

After about a three-month hiatus after the Founding Fathers talk, Michael invited Ray back. Michael had realized this root, this wedge, would hinder us going forward until it was removed. Pastor McMillian was the surgeon for the job.

Our first meeting with Ray back was pivotal. He shared a newsletter from a prominent national white evangelical highlighting Thomas Jefferson and George Washington as "heroes" for the church. As if by a revelational work of the Holy Spirit and Ray's truth-speaking, this time, it all clicked. It made sense, and something like a second conversion took place for the white leaders that day, including me.

From that day forward, we agreed to meet twice monthly, one meeting for going deeper relationally and one for the work of pulling up the wedge of unchecked nationalism in the American church.

The first Thursday of the month gathering became an intentional cross-racial covenant group, a sharing group, a life-group that continues to this day. The second Thursday of the month group was the antecedent for what later became Race to Unity, founded by Ray McMillian.

The work for Race to Unity in the days ahead, from 1999 forward, would be fast and furious, powerful and life-changing; the work in our covenant group would be deep and relational. A lot of us were in both groups—and still are.

Chapter 44

DISMANTLING IDOLATRY IN THE CHURCH

By late 1999, we soon realized that Pastor Ray was an equal opportunity agitator. Not only would he not allow white believers off the hook on unchecked nationalism, he wouldn't let black leaders off the hook on over-spiritualizing Civil Rights–era leaders who were not gospel-centered.

Together, black and white church leaders in Cincinnati were being confronted with truth that was setting us free and allowing us to unite as the church. This resulted in my own life becoming more racially prepared as, in 2000, I entered a year of transition toward lead-pastoring First Christian Assembly of God into a reconciling future, reconciling people to the Father and one another through Jesus Christ, and none other.

As I shared earlier, not until 2004 did I feel ready and stirred by the Holy Spirit to directly address this nationalism subject in the church, as I did on Sunday, July 4. But in the city, Race to Unity was soon to invite national evangelical leaders, black and white, to consider this topic together. Those leaders would include Tony Evans, Bill Hybels, T. D. Jakes, Max Lucado, John M. Perkins, James Robeson, George Yancy, Michael Emerson, and many others.

Ray was called, like an Old Testament prophet to the people of God, to be a prophetic message bearer to the twenty-first-century church in the United States, to show "the house to the house," like Ezekiel (Ezekiel 43:10 KJV).

Amazingly, the American gospel-centered church would be awakening to a deep, stretching racial reconciliation work.

Church-as-heaven-on-earth as one new humanity (Ephesians 2:15; John 17:21) was becoming conceptually plausible even in the deepest divide in the American church—the black/white fissure. But this would happen only if we were willing to deal with the wedge, the root of racism in the church—over-spiritualized American history and unchecked patriotism.

Chapter 45

CITY SERVANTS

By the mid-2000s, the racial and interdenominational unity in the church of Cincinnati was yielding the kind of mutuality and teamwork we could only faintly dream of at that watershed 1998 leaders gathering when Bishop Dwight Wilkins bared his soul.

A shared gospel-centered group emerged. It would become known as City Servants and would consist of women and men, white, black, and brown, Jew and Gentile, marketplace Christian lay leaders and clergy, parachurch and local church leaders. These men and women love Jesus and one another and are covenanted for maximum impact across our region in evangelism and outcome-based biblical justice work, prayer and proclamation, church multiplication, and discipleship. They are pro-life, from the womb to the tomb. This the whole church ministering the whole gospel in all parts of the city, together, in unity.

In 2017, we published a statement:

The Statement of Commitment to Unity
We are followers of Jesus from many different traditions—historic protestant, Catholic, nondenomenational, Messianic Jewish, and more—who are committing to love, peace, unity, and justice. We believe loving God and loving others are highest priorities. We are excited about the growing commitment to one another that we are witnessing in the greater Cincinnati area and beyond, both inside and

outside the four walls of the church and across racial, ethnic, denominational, and economic lines.

Over the past few years, we have seen cooperation in the spirit of service and justice among groups as diverse as AMOS, City Servants, the Catholic Archdiocese, Transformation Cincinnati and Northern Kentucky, the Beacon of Hope Business Alliance, City Gospel Mission, the CityLink Center, Whole Again, Crossroads Church, and dozens of other congregations and faith leaders around our city. We are eager to continue to work together so followers of Jesus can truly be a source of hope and promise in our city. In this spirit:

» we commit to respect our various theological differences and institutional priorities while working together in ways that advance God's Kingdom for all;

» we commit to put aside personal agendas for the greater purpose of serving God and each other as we learn to humble ourselves before God and submit to one another;

» we commit to treat each other with respect, patience, understanding, humility, grace, and mercy as we love and forgive each other unconditionally;

» we commit to eliminate gossip from our conversations and prayer times;

» we commit to resolving any interpersonal differences with one another quickly and in humility, love, forgiveness, and truth, following the pattern given by Christ Himself in Matthew 18.

We acknowledge that Jesus' call to love is irrevocable, that we are better together than we are apart, and that no one has all the answers. We cannot accomplish what God desires for this city, nation, and world unless we model the love of Christ and work together on a much deeper level of unity and commitment to the lordship of Christ. Believing this is God's call, we invite all followers of Christ to add their names to this commitment.

This statement is posted at UnifyCincy.com.

We placed it as a full-page ad in our Cincinnati papers, the *Herald* (African American owned) and the *Cincinnati Enquirer*. Over 150 leaders signed it.

Nineteen years of work. Nineteen years together. Nineteen years toward healing.

Dwight's heart expression in 1998 was where it all began. Now we are at work together. The city will not be the same. We still have a long way to go, but we're moving. We're moving together. We are jars of clay but filled with living water.

Along the way, our churches have changed.

Peoples Church is just one example. But greater Cincinnati now has many multiracial/multi-ethnic/multi-economic churches, under black, brown, and white leadership. these churches and ministries, diversely united and rooted in the Kingdom and anchored by the gospel, are loving all people wholeheartedly into Christ and into the fellowship of the believers and addressing harmful systems and ills head on as microcosms of the one new humanity people of God whom Jesus paid for on the Cross (Ephesians 2:15; Revelation 5:9-10).

Chapter 46

MLB AND RACIAL JUSTICE SUMMIT

Again and again, the Lord keeps astounding us with surprises.

In May 2015, believers in Cincinnati hosted a Freedom Summit, combining two dynamic biblical justice conversations in our nation: racial justice and human trafficking. The summit was facilitated by the National Underground Railroad Freedom Center.

In the middle of the conference, a handful of racially diverse and gospel-centered pastors realizing that the Major League Baseball All-Star Game soon coming to Cincinnati would provide a ready platform for educating around racial justice. So we held a press conference one block from the Freedom Center in front of Great American Ballpark where the All-Star Game was soon to be held. That year in America, the social media and national news platforms news frequently reported police brutality against young black men at an alarming rate.

Just months before, Ferguson and Baltimore had been burning. Would the MLB consider seizing the moment, and their national All-Star Game stage, to raise substantive dialogue? Had it not been for the white supremacist hecklers at our press conference, our statements may have gone largely unnoticed. The heated shouting by the fascist group created enough concern within MLB that before long we were together with MLB execs, the Reds brass, the Freedom Center leadership, and local clergy planning what emerged as an outstanding several-hour event Friday night of the 2015 All-Star Game weekend. MLB video recorded the event and, as of this writing, still holds that amazing content on their website.

Who would have thought? Prophetic action, out of reconciling relationships, rooted in a reconciling gospel, impacting on a national stage. How hungry our country really is for honest and earnest truth and reconciliation conversations. Ephesians 2:15 churches and diversely united gospel leaders can help catalyze and lead the way.

Chapter 47

NPR

Later that same year, as the nation was reeling from alleged racialized police brutality episodes, the media came looking for new stories, good news stories. Once again, national reporters were interviewing Peoples Church Cincinnati members, asking what they were experiencing and how it was impacting their lives. In print, the story read like this, "How a Once-White Church Broke Down Racial Barriers." To me, clearly, the Lord was using church-as-heaven-on-earth for a national stage to share a big part of what He's about, reconciling people to Himself and to one another and healing the nation's ills through His costly blood-work on the Cross.

Why do I share this? Because I want you to see that your city needs a new story. Your community, and our nation, needs good news stories, gospel stories. These stories will bring many to the King and His Kingdom, and the fruit out of your church will help increase the harvest in your community. Remember, Peoples Church Cincinnati is a middle-sized church in a middle-sized city in a Midwest state. But the story is powerful. Imagine there being hundreds, thousands of these stories across the United States. That would be nothing short of salt and light.

Chapter 48

TA NEHISI COATES

While on sabbatical in early 2016, I experienced a divine encounter like when the Lord called me onto my face in prayer about our church name change.

I was in a southern California condo on the beach enjoying a wintertime respite in the sun, praying, resting, reading, and writing.

Some years before, my sister Kelli had sent me an *Atlantic* article by Ta Nehisi Coates, "The Case for Reparations." I had delayed reading it because it seemed intense and was long. But on sabbatical by myself for a few days, I felt stirred to pull out the piece. As I read, I cried. I was moved so deeply I couldn't put it down. In fact, I kept reading portions of it over and over—the detail, the facts, and the impact of Coates's prophetic voice pierced my heart. As I read, I began to hear the quiet, gentle voice of the Holy Spirit saying something to me that seemed crazy-dangerous—something that would be unquestionably unpopular for sure.

"Chris, I want white evangelicals, under African American evangelical mentoring, to lift their voices together to address this matter of unrealized repentance as a nation." I wept. How could this possibly ever happen? Whites hate to hear the word "reparations," responding with almost a visceral repulsion, as if we are going to be cheated of all that we are. The feeling is irrational but powerful.

I suddenly remembered a meeting from the early 2000s at Oak Cliff Church's youth center, where Dr. Tony Evans is pastor. A few national church leaders had gathered in Dallas to ask the question: "What will it take to heal racism in the church?"

At a point in the meeting, one of the older, white leaders stood up to push back on what he thought was a tasteless direction to the talks, "If this meeting is about reparations, I'm out of here." It wasn't, and the comment made no sense at the time in light of the discussions taking place; but it made an imprint on me. White Christians hate any hint of reparations talk for the sin of slavery in America.

Now I was reading Coates's ground-shaking article, and the Holy Spirit was stirring a vision in me to help give leadership to that very thing. For five hours I read, I grieved, and I listened as best I could. And I shook my head. This was impossible.

The next day, I was flying home through the Denver airport. At one point during my long layover, I decided to try and find a local coffee shop. As I passed through an intersection between terminals, someone intentionally bumped into me. It was my friend Jason Janz! We had participated together in a two-year Leadership Network, their first for a multi-ethnic church. What were the odds? But what he said almost immediately after a good laugh and a short greeting stunned me. "Chris, you said something two years ago that I just can't shake. You said, 'We've never as a nation apologized for slavery.'" Of all the topics Jason could have brought up with me in our fifteen minutes before we boarded our respective flights, the very day after I read Ta Nehisi Coates's article, he said *that*?

I reached into my bag and pulled out the dog-eared *Atlantic* article that had so keenly gripped my heart. "Jason, let me tell you what I was hearing in my spirit just yesterday." Jason nodded as he listened and then interjected, "This is God, and it needs to be framed biblically as 'restitution.'" We briefly brainstormed next steps and were off to our jetways. This initiative still lies dormant, but I know God is in it.

Chapter 49

DR. MARK FAIRCHILD

Along this journey I can't tell you how many times "divine appointments," as my dad used to call them, or what you might think of simply as God moments, have shockingly occurred.

An exceptional such occurrence came just after my sabbatical trip to the archeological site of Ephesus in early 2016. In chapter 4, I shared how after lunch the tour guide showed us the site of St. John's Basilica, the traditional burial site of the youngest of the twelve disciples. The weightiness of learning that John had finished his ministry pastoring this church, and from the city of Ephesus, was discussed in Part 1 of this book. What I didn't share, however, was what happened at the Basilica site that day.

During the entire tour that morning, our Turkish guide had been singing the praises of New Testament scholar and archeology buff Dr. Mark Fairchild, an evangelical scholar and professor at Huntington University who specializes in Asia Minor early church studies. While taking pictures near John's burial spot, I noticed a group of Americans approaching. Our guide suddenly exclaimed, "There's Dr. Fairchild!"

Within moments we were talking, and Mark asked about Cincinnati. "My daughter recently was there for a couple years. Do you know the church, Crossroads?"

I smiled broadly, "Of course. Our relationship goes back to their very beginning." I explained briefly what all was stirring in my heart that day and invited myself to visit him back home to talk further. Later that summer, Mark graciously shared two days of time together with me as we dove deeply into many of the thoughts included in this book. That's when he told me of his archeological discoveries of early church worship sites in southern Turkey with Jewish and Gentile inscriptions on the façades, evidence of mixed ethnic inclusion.

Leaving his home after two exhilarating days of fellowship, sharing, and prayer, I marveled at the intensity and extraordinary detail of the Lord's effort to give assurances that He was in this process for getting out His message underscoring His vision of church-as-heaven-on-earth. He already had many key leaders and thinkers with different pieces of the puzzle who would help illustrate the mystery of Christ now being revealed (see Ephesians 3:4-6).

PART V

Praxis

In this section, I want to share some practical ideas that are in no way definitive or exhaustive. And at the end of the book, you'll find resources to consider. As an emerging practitioner yourself, maybe in time you will write and add to what the church needs in the decades ahead.

Here are questions I want to respond to next:

» How did we work out this vision in our family life?
» What are lessons we learned and tools we use at Peoples Church Cincinnati?
» What are lessons and tools for us in the church of Greater Cincinnati, the church collective?

PRAXIS—PERSONAL LIFE

Chapter 50

DIVERSIFYING OUR OWN LIVES

It was essential to my wife, Jan, and me that our personal lives grew in and exhibited racial and cultural inclusion—not just for us, but for our kids, too.

Unlike me, Jan had grown up in a school community rich in ethnic, economic, and racial diversity. Princeton schools in Cincinnati could provide our kids this richly diverse environment and solid academics at the same time. We bought our first home in this school district.

We also realized that our entertainment needed to be diverse. Our personal tastes in music, the arts, history, foods, and the like would by necessity be enlarged as we intentionally stretched and exposed ourselves and our palates to forms different than our defaults.

This includes television programming, radio selection, movie choices, book authors and topics, eating out experiences, and naturally, intentional new friendships in our lives.

We just began listening and paying attention to possibilities that would enlarge our worldview, our understanding, and our exposure to cultures beyond our own family of origin or preference choices.

At the risk of redundancy, let me say again that it just made sense that if we increased our intercultural vocabulary and widened the scope of our life perspective, tastes, likes, and spectrum of familiar, we would be more ethnically and culturally versatile. Also, we would raise our "ethnic IQ" for attracting, engaging, and retaining new friends and church family, people unlike ourselves.

I remember asking friends of color about the worship music they liked and the artists they regularly listened to. I talked about my new experiences as illustrations in my preaching. Along the way, folks in the congregation began to help me with what they, too, were learning and benefiting from in their intentional cross-racial, cross-cultural experiences.

I still remember the business woman in the church handing me a copy of Randy Alcorn's novel, *Dominion*, which had captivated her attention. The story includes a cross-racial friendship wherein so many normal and natural aspects of life were shared between the lead characters. I can still recall specifically how the book stirred in me a desire to try "soul food" and to play more jazz music in my car and at home.

During one season, I devoured a Ken Burns documentary on jazz music and was astounded at all the black history I still did not know. Even today, I'm discovering much more, and my life is being enriched.

When I overheard a friend of color laughing about a line in a comedy titled *Barbershop*, I rented the movie. When the National Underground Railroad Freedom Center opened in our city to much fanfare and excitement, I decided to go as often as I could and carefully learn as much as my mind and heart could process in each visit. I still go. Like great art, you can gain enrichment from every viewing. We invited African American friends into our home for small group. We went to one another's birthday parties and shared dinner, life, and laughs.

All along the way, we grew. And we grew as reconcilers.

As the church diversified, our children's friendships did as well. Our house was frequently full of diverse groups of young people as the kids matured into their teen years. From school and from church alike, the Beard kids were living authentic racially and ethnically inclusive lives, something I personally didn't experience as I grew up in mostly mono-ethnic, mono-economic environments.

Church-like-heaven-on-earth was personal for us, and others could feel the authenticity. This was deep in our souls, implanted by our heavenly Father and welcomed by our own hearts through His grace and with the Spirit's help.

My cross-racial covenant group of pastors swapped life-stories and cultural experiences; we were learning from each other. At least twice every month, year after year, I had a place to process with diverse friends, brothers in Christ, all I was learning—and they lovingly stretched me even further.

Things got to where if on vacation I visited a homogeneous church, it felt incomplete. Our personal lives were hungry for the every tribe, language, and nation church.

This didn't mean things were always comfortable or easy. Things weren't.

At times we made mistakes. We lost friends for short seasons and long seasons. Sometimes friends of the lighter hue, like us, didn't understand what we were about now. And sometimes our new friends were the ones who might question our sincerity when we made unwitting mistakes with them. Though these latter experiences of being questioned about our sincerity were few and far between, they did happen.

Jesus never promised easy. He just said, "Follow me." We were convinced that this new direction for us was where He wanted us going and where He had always been.

Chapter 51

MUSIC AND MOVIES

Whenever I ride in the car of one of my friends of a different ethnicity, I pay attention to what music he's playing on his car stereo. I make a mental note and download it as soon as possible for my own enjoyment. Naturally, at times he won't be listening to an artist of color but not often. Through this method I came across Lecrae, Tedashii, Trip Lee, Donnie McClurkin, Nicole C. Mullen, and Ben Tankard, for Christian examples, but also great jazz artists and pop artists not yet in Christ. In the beginning, I listened to DC Talk and later TobyMac, a white artist, clued in to racial reconciliation. DC Talk's 1995 project, "Jesus Freak," with its song "Colored People" was seminal for me, as was TobyMac's "Welcome to Diverse City" project. More recently I have been encouraged by the inclusion work of Elevation, Mosaic MSC, and Hillsong.

Include other new young artists in your listening for church worship—artists of color and ethnicity different than yours. For me, that means leaders like Travis Greene and Tye Tribbett. Now I'm also branching to African and Latin music expressions. My life is so enriched! And it enriches our congregation as I can relate to our members more effectively as a result. Music gets in your being. Your tastes can increase. As proof, I can also now enjoy some new country and folk music, indie rock, and dance music.

As for movies—the first time I watched *Antwone Fisher* on an overseas flight, I cried. My heart was touched so deeply. Then I saw *Twelve Years a Slave*, *Amistad*, and *Selma* just to name a few. I also took in the comedy *Barbershop*. Adding these to my childhood television experiences of *Roots*, *The*

Jeffersons, and *Good Times*, I had quite a lot of exposure to black and American history that opened my life to basic understanding not otherwise received in my homogeneous, white upbringing. Today I enjoy watching *Black-ish* for a contemporary take on the American black experience. All of these are vicarious and don't take the place of real-life friendships, but they do add content for deep conversations as well as for lamenting and celebrating, laughing and mutual sharing—rich enjoyment in all my friendships.

Chapter 52

FRIENDS

INTENTIONAL FRIENDSHIPS

My first friendship with a Christian brother who is African American happened when I was twenty-eight. I mean a real friend. Galen Jones and I were introduced through a mutual friend who knew we had similar passions about Kingdom things. We're still friends today. Galen's special-needs brother is part of our congregation. Peoples Church folk love him so well. Galen leads Kingdom things in the deep South now, but our friendship that started in 1995 was life-changing for me.

Together we traveled in November of 1995 to a meeting of church leaders from a hundred cities gathering in Los Angeles to discuss and strategize the vision of reaching the city through a cooperative effort by the Body of Christ. Galen was the only man of color in the meeting of two hundred or so. On that trip, as we roomed together to save on cost, I learned about life through my brother's lenses. And my life was not the same after that.

I heard for the first time the reality of what "shopping while black" can be like (being followed by store detectives) or "driving while black" (vulnerable to being pulled over for no reason other than your skin color making you seem suspicious). I learned that two Americas exists—one for African Americans and one for those of the lighter hues. Not to say that we don't have many Americas, but on that trip, this was all new to me; and I was rocked to learn not everyone has the same American experience.

How naive, right? But true. It was 1995. As I already shared in Part II, in 1998, I entered intentional cross-racial friendships with several other pastors of our city. Galen was my initial introducer to each of them. Today I enjoy many friendships with brothers and sisters of color, and many not yet in Christ. I actually began by sharing my heart burden for racial reconciliation with white friends, which then led to black friendships through their networks. That's how I met Galen.

CROSS-RACIAL, COVENANT GROUP

Our covenant group has now been meeting for twenty years. We've slowed down to quarterly, even semi-annually some years, as life has moved some of us on and health has declined for a few. At fifty-one, I'm our youngest member.

I love these men. They are dear to me. We've shared hundreds of hours over coffee and Diet Cokes, meals, weddings, and funerals; we've cried together, argued, laughed, sat in silence, counseled one another, prayed for each other, and shared our innermost hearts with each other as deeply as I have with anyone except my wife, Jan. We are in covenant until we meet Jesus.

More than any other vehicle in my life, this small group for life has informed my vision for church-as-heaven-on-earth. I can't recommend the idea enough.

Chapter 53

REFLECTION

WHAT I LEARNED ON MY SABBATICAL

The year 2016 began for me with a seven-week sabbatical that was life-altering in many good ways. For one, I had time to stop, rest, and reflect.

The church had been through a massive overhaul, with numerous inputs, outputs, and concussive experiences, both exhilarating and life-giving but also at times brutal and injurious throughout the entire fifteen years of personal and church transformation. Those high-energy impacts simply take a toll that perhaps only stopping cold reveals.

The first week I simply rested. I slept as much as I wanted to, and I decompressed. The church had allowed me to put in place a terrific plan for complete detachment, so my mind was truly able to be free. After plentiful rest, I took some days to reflect and listen to the Lord about the significance of all we had been through, and what He now wanted in us and from us as the Beards and as Peoples Church.

On one of my seven West Coast beach days during February that year, I felt drawn to the book of Ephesians, again and again. Later at a Kentucky monastery, Abbey of Gethsemani, I would write the initial article that would later lead to the theology at the beginning of this book. Someone had pointed me to Gethsemane, where Thomas Merton had lived, worked, and written profoundly for the church of Jesus Christ in the earth. How inspiring and awe-inducing it was to think I was typing my first words at the same hilly, quiet campus. Again and again as I wrote, I sensed the Holy Spirit guiding the emphasis of the mystery of Christ as defined in Ephesians 2 and 3.

All of this was happening before I was aware that later in the sabbatical I'd be standing at the archeological site of Ephesus in western Turkey. That simply was divine arrangement.

On this sabbatical I learned some new truths for me: (1) how closely the Spirit really does guide our steps. Jeremiah 10:23 says, "Lord, I know that people's lives are not their own; it is not for them to direct their steps" (what a trust in God is gained from that knowing); (2) the richness gained from rest and reflection for delivering fresh ministry (Henri Nouwen, *The Way of the Heart*); and (3) the gift of turning off your email after 6 p.m. every day, from then on. Simple lessons that have changed my life.

BOOKS

If I had another fifty years just to read, I'm not sure I could read every book I have on my heart to read. So choosing wisely as I go with the years I have left is very important to me. I want to focus on books that will enlarge my being, my mind, and my understanding and enrich my life for better serving the King and His Kingdom. And that barely helps limit the list. But it does; so in addition to the extravagant time in His Word that roots life and ministry, I want to be a voracious reader. My sabbath helped me get back to that. (See some of these in the Resource List at the back of this book.)

NOURISHING OUR MARRIAGE

Jan and I are called as a one-flesh couple to the work of the Lord in the earth, starting with our family, our local church, our city, and then beyond. But after the crucial priority years of raising our incredible kids and pouring our all into them, we now joyously enjoy sharing together in leading Peoples Church Cincinnati and Network and celebrating each other under Christ.

Ephesians 5:21 calls us, husbands and wives, as believers, to be mutually submitted to each other. It then spells out what that means in their respective roles to each other. Every day is a laboratory of growth for Jan and me in those assignments, but here's what I know: As we lean into the gift of each other and cultivate the good, share in the good, and receive from the good in each other for our union, we feel the smile of heaven and experience the protection and counsel of the Lord through one another.

We still get tired and cranky with each other of course, but we also linger there less. I've learned that the leadership gifts in Jan powerfully complement my own in ways I'm discovering daily; so together we're able to do more, do deeper, and dream longer into the future. Our mornings together often begin with side-by-side devotions, and our days end with lots of touch and affection. The health of our marriage is a microcosm for the health of our ministry. These are things we are learning over time and still growing in.

FASTING, REFINING

Without regular fasting and prayer, I'm not sure one can lead truly game-changing, significant ministry. Why? Because the spiritual battle is so real, so intense, so schemed. Fasting humbles us. Fasting lowers our flesh and increases our forward movement. Fasting intensifies our prayer life and sharpens our spirit. The Kingdom of darkness fights hard and fights unfair. Fasting helps us be wiser and keeps us lighter of foot spiritually so as not to be outschemed by the evil one or unnecessarily injured in combat (2 Corinthians 2:11). (See Resource List.)

WORSHIP

Whether with music or in silence, in quiet prayer or verbal praise, lifting my heart to the Father daily for extended times of lavishing my love on Him and receiving His for me are essential. Journaling, reflecting, rejoicing, interceding, prostrating and standing, and kneeling and sitting—extravagant time with Jesus.

FUN

I personally like to golf, and together, Jan and I love a great movie, a captivating streamed TV series, or a long walk enjoying each other's quiet company. Fun, laughter, and recreation refuel our very beings more than we know. The seriousness of our work, its implications for heaven and hell, requires that we also *live*, enjoying the fresh air of an evening walk, mountain stream fishing, or the crashing waves at a sun-soaked beach. We have to mix in fun to renew our souls.

These are the matters of personal praxis that have changed my life and allowed me to experience flourishing while battling the gates of hell through Christ in us. Christ wins. The church wins. We win.

PRAXIS—LOCAL CHURCH

Chapter 54

BASICS FOR LEADING A LOCAL CHURCH INTO A DIVERSE UNITY

THEOLOGY

First things first—root the work in Scripture. Anything else is shifting sand. Hence the first few chapters of this book.

THE 70/30 RULE

Let people know that a percentage of what's going on in a diversely united church they won't ever personally choose. But the song they dislike, the event they don't appreciate, the sermon illustration they don't understand, the perspective they don't see, and the language use they don't like is bringing tears of joy and the experience of inclusion and belonging to someone else in the church family, not to mention might be reaching a new person with the gospel who's "getting it" for the first time. Seventy percent ministers to you, and 30 percent is for the vision of the Jesus-bought church. I have no scientific backing for this, just a gut sense of what it takes, what it's like, and how to explain it to people. We share this out loud in our services from time to time. This flies in the face of consumer-based church strategy, or easy growth, but neither was Christ's incarnation easy (Philippians 2).

TIME

Timeliness is no more next to godliness than is homogeneity. Not that time doesn't matter; it does. It's just used differently in different cultures. So, in culturally inclusive churches, especially mutually agreed-upon and communicated expectations around start and end times in church life (services, weddings, funerals, social events, etc.) is very important. But the value of Western promptness is more cultural than spiritual. What *is* spiritual is figuring out common agreements to honor in a diverse church. For weddings, we ask, "Will this wedding start on workday time or traditional time?" And then we carefully and respectfully spread the word. Sometimes the event itself, the full experience of it as unpressured by time, is the higher value than Euro-based promptness. Good communication, flexibility among cultures, understanding, good humor, and mutual respect are the keys to nourish and enjoy unity with regard to how time is used

MUTUAL HUMILITY, MUTUAL RESPECT

People can sense when they are respected or merely tolerated. Know the difference; live the difference as a body of believers.

WHEN FEARFUL, PERSEVERE

Fear is crippling. It will set you back. It will disrupt what God wants. Never let fear win: fear of failure, fear of loss, fear of cost. You will have pangs of fear along the way. Persevere through the fear. Trust that the living God wants this even more than you do, and that He can correct and redeem your mistakes. Mistakes are inevitable but not determinative. In the end, Jesus wins. You win. We win. We are His. Stay obedient to the work of the gospel.

WHEN OPPOSED, TEACH GENTLY

Don't assume that people know what they are objecting to or about. They may simply be undergoing culture shock and shift and simply need the Word gently offered, time to think on it, and the opportunity to ask questions without feeling attacked. I was terrible at doing this well in the early years of our work. I was often reactionary and too impassioned and didn't listen well or long enough for people to feel heard. I would jump to teaching too fast. You will do better.

FAST AND PRAY

Understand that your real opposition is spiritual and must be spiritually fought. Add a weekly day of fasting and prayer to your life. If not for twenty-four hours, do eighteen-hour fasts, evening meal to evening meal. Or some other regimen, but weekly. Fight the fight with spiritual weapons.

Invite a weekly or monthly corporate prayer meeting, even if it's just a handful of believers who regularly fight the fight through prayer over you, the church, and the work of His Kingdom advancing. God has those in the church who will pray. When taking new territory of any kind as a church, invite people to volunteer and take a day of the week to fast for a set season. Consider beginning each year with a week or more of fasting and prayer. Gather the whole church together for at least one evening or morning of that time, all who will come for this hard work, to seek the Lord together. Teach the church how to war from their knees with fasting.

Read anything and everything on prayer and fasting by Jim Cymbala, Timothy Keller, John Piper, Jentezen Franklin, Tony Evans, Richard Foster, and others. And this is important: See Ephesians 6, the most developed spiritual armor and battle chapter of the Bible, through the lens of Ephesians 2:15, 3:6, 9-10. Reading those texts helps make sense of why Paul and the Holy Spirit place this teaching on spiritual battle, how to defend and fight in it, in this epistle. See the spiritual warfare realities and truths expounded in Ephesians 6 as especially predicated on the work of the diversely united church expounded on in Ephesians 1–5.

SHARED POWER, SHARED DECISION-MAKING

Everyone working toward an inclusive multiethnic, multieconomic future in the local church knows you must have a visibly diverse stage, hospitality ministry, and digital media showing your vision of diverse unity and inclusion. What a lot of churches and ministries are painfully missing is this: genuinely shared decision-making, authentically shared power. What decisions are made with only the dominant church group in the room? How are directional decisions initiated? Finalized? How are vision, goals, objectives, staffing, budget prioritization, and strategic decisions made? Who is in the room?

» What is the structure of your board? Your staff? Your elders? Beyond structure, do you make it drop-dead, nonnegotiable essential that every important decision in the church has at least a microcosm of your major groups present, even if just among two or three people?

» Mutuality is felt at this level. You either really have it, or you don't. And if you don't, you are not where you should be. The deeper diverse unity that I think exhibits the manifold wisdom of heaven on earth and its concomitant declarations to principalities and powers (Ephesians 3:9-10) is still developing for you. Power imbalances cross-racially and cross-culturally still need to be explored and solved.

» The "inefficiency" of this priority screams against the speed often wanted for growth and energy stewardship. But so do the laws of the harvest (see Stephen Covey's 7 *Habits of Highly Effective People*).

DEEP TRUST AT A DIVERSE LEADERSHIP CORE

Just to underscore the prior principle: your senior leadership, the last persons in the room for making critical decisions, probably has to be one or two people more than what seems smart for efficient decision-making, or that you might personally prefer. But without the diverse inclusion needed to share power, you will short-circuit the shared unity and potential wisdom for the whole that you really want, that I think He wants in His church. You need heart-level, life trust in and love for one another. The rest of the staff, volunteer or paid, and the congregation itself can feel if this really does exist or not. So you can't cut corners on this.

Thus, the senior leader's own life has to be trustworthy in this respect. Regardless of the titles people carry, find a way to include in that final deciding team the mega-groups of the church. I really see this as nonnegotiable, and getting there will require failures and grace, humility and affirmations—losses grieved and wins celebrated—all of this building one on the other, forging deep trust. It requires pouring into one another's lives outside of the normal work flow. Retreats, hanging out together, and shared experiences enhance this quality of relationship and trust. Your consistency and keeping commitments to one another as diverse leaders is what will create the content for this level of trust and unity.

GET COMFORTABLE WITH THE UNCOMFORTABLE

Model and teach this principle, story this principle, celebrate this principle! Say things like, "At Peoples Church we challenge ourselves to get comfortable with the uncomfortable." Why? Because unsurrendered comfort and selfish personal preferences are the enemies of diverse unity. The flesh has to die continually to be and do church-as-heaven-on-earth. Whoever said church experience is supposed to be comfortable anyway, a rest from the scary world? Who in the Bible ever said that? No one! The New Testament authors, over and over, talk about taking up our cross, bearing with one another. We sorrow and we rejoice. We find joy in the richness of all the "one-anotherings" the church is called to, but comfort is never promised. Did Jesus Himself not leave His omnipresent privilege to confine Himself to an incarnate experience for the rest of eternity on our behalf? And we're called His followers.

REDEFINE CONSERVATIVE AND LIBERAL BIBLICALLY

One of the greatest challenges for the evangelical church in America for discovering and walking in the mystery of Christ (one new humanity, Jew and Gentile, black and white, male and female, rich and poor—Ephesians 3:4-6) are the partisan political activity and the definitions of conservative and liberal. What if our definition of conservative actually meant scriptural faithfulness, obedience, adherence, and rootedness instead of the worldly political category of "right wing"? How might this make us different?

Well, for one, we would be pro-life *from the womb to the tomb*, and we wouldn't see that as being worldly liberal but as biblical. We wouldn't waffle on sexual morality in the church because love and grace toward people would include the truth in love, not the absence of truth or what can be just as bad, truth *without* love. Nor would we waffle on gossip, slander, or un-Christlike attitudes toward pre-believers. This would be what it is to be conservative, liberal with love, biblically anchored, equal parts truth and love, unpoliticized. We would care as much about societal righteousness and biblical justice as we do personal holiness for the believer.

James 1:27, for an example, would be a key verse for this two-part faithfulness we walk in and model: caring for orphans and widows in their distress while *also* keeping ourselves from being polluted by the world. Redefining the word "conservative" biblically, not politically, helps the church look, feel, walk, and talk more like Jesus and less like a judgmental and disconnected subculture mislabeled as "evangelical." If we don't make this step, we risk staying monoethnic, monoeconomic, aging, and eventually dying. We need biblical conservatism, not political conservatism; biblical liberality, not secular, and we need to know the difference.

DEPOLITICIZE YOUR PULPIT

This is not to say don't use your voice regarding current events and matters of biblical justice that require a loving, godly perspective; just don't side with candidates or parties from the pulpit. Be an equal-opportunity agitator and an equal-opportunity grace-sharer. And maybe more important than anything else said in this paragraph, be as passionate about racism and racial injustice as you are about abortion, biblical sexuality, or gay marriage, and vice versa. Have all your public stands, or "elephant in the room" talks soaked in humility and love. Anything less has the feel to newcomers that you are partisan and unfairly partial, judgmental, or hateful.

Sin and injustice are sin and injustice. We can't have pet categories as the church. To do so is more American than it is Christian. Do you really want only to be working to reach half of society with the gospel? That's what you're doing if you have a politicized or partisan pulpit. You're placing your politics, or those of your majority congregational group, as a hurdle between them and many minority members, many lost people, many guests, and many in your community and in some respects, between them and the Cross of Jesus Christ. Since we are ambassadors here of a different Kingdom, we represent a different government. This is not our home, and we're here to be salt and light to all. All means *all*.

Everybody in a Group

Every group diverse. Once the congregation is diversifying through inclusion of diverse members, work toward experiencing that richness at the small group and serving team levels of church life. Though it might seem counterintuitive to the diversely united church, minority and immigrant groups need to have refuel times together with others in the body who have shared societal experience, challenges, or language, but these are exactly for that: refueling and strengthening for the greater work of diverse unity, one new humanity, diversely united house of God flourishing. In Acts 6, we see that the Grecian Jewish part of the body felt concerned about their widows receiving equal treatment. This seems to indicate that people were talking and sharing together in subgroups from time to time. Yet, the goal was to solve problems for the health of all as one.

Skittles

At Peoples Church Cincinnati, we actually have annual "all-in" small group sessions lasting four to six weeks. We intentionally, and with fun, vision-cast everybody in a group, every group diverse, like a bag of Skittles! We actually have folks sign up using Skittles-colored felt markers representing mega-groups in the body—Latino, African American, Caucasian, East African, West African, Asian, etc. The colors are random, and they help us organize diversely in order to share in and celebrate our richness together. We also theme our life groups like this: small groups are where we live and learn the Kingdom *together*.

Specific Curricula

At times, we intentionally study the Word of God and reconciliation, diversity, economic inclusion, culture, biblical and racial justice, as well as many other gospel-centered and discipleship themes. But those times when we go all in diversely together for "Crossonomics," "Multi-ethnic Conversations," or "Undivided" are church-wide experiences through fellowship and study that deepen the work of Ephesians 2:21-22 in us: "In him the whole building is joined together and rises to become a holy temple in the Lord. And in him you too are being built together to become a dwelling in which God lives by his Spirit." These groups have more naturally reflected church-like-heaven-on-earth, but intentional initiatives ensure that it's happening—especially for all the new people coming in but also for the rest of us.

ADDRESS CROSS-RACIAL/ETHNIC DATING AND MARRIAGE

I keenly remember the first time we talked this topic at Peoples. I had recently heard Pastor Fred Price teach on it from Numbers 12, the story of Miriam despising Moses' Cushite wife, a woman of color. Pastor Price leaned into the story with vigor: "You want white, I'll give you white!" he exclaimed as he impersonated God's interaction with Miriam just before striking her with leprosy after her racist complaint. I knew in my spirit that until I talked openly about this same subject from Scripture, some in the body would resist the vision.

Soon after that 2004 or 2005 Sunday when I taught Price's message almost verbatim, while giving him credit, an older, influential man in the body visited my office. He was sincerely concerned about the implications of that Numbers 12 sermon. "Chris, the Bible says, 'What does light have to do with dark?'"

Astounded, yet helped by the Holy Spirit, with compassion welling up in my heart for this man I'd known since my childhood, I opened the Scriptures to the text he was referencing. After I read, "Do not be yoked together with unbelievers. For what do righteousness and wickedness have in common? Or what fellowship can light have with darkness?" (2 Corinthians 6:14), he sighed, "Oh." For a few moments we just looked at each other, then he said, "Well, pastor, I still think we're going to have problems with that." Although he recognized that the passage refers to right relationships between believers and unbelievers, he still couldn't accept the idea of interracial dating and marriage. Sad.

That whole interaction, and all the weight it might have carried still to this day brings a rise to my eyebrows. To his credit, the man is still in the church, and he lovingly serves everyone equally in his volunteer roles. Not long after that office visit, our church began to see an influx of interracial couples; and many years later my daughter married a young man of color raised in the church, profoundly enriching our lives and family.

COMPLEXITY AND SIMPLICITY

In church-as-heaven-on-earth, you have to hold with equal emphasis the values of efficiency and diverse inclusion. One value can't give way to the other or there is loss. If you eliminate the value of simplicity at the cost of diverse inclusion, you will struggle to scale, to grow. But if you allow simplicity, the value of efficiency, to overrule diverse inclusion, then the blood-bought purchase of Jesus will suffer. Pursue these values with equal vigor at all times.

INCLUSION AND EXCELLENCE

Similarly, the values of inclusion and excellence must have equal importance. In fact, I recommend you make the inclusion value inherent in your idea of excellence. Excellence is a Kingdom value, and so is diverse inclusion. One can't overrule the other, so allow for the laws of the harvest. Your idea of excellence, with diverse inclusion, will sometimes have to be cultivated over more time than you would like. I recommend that you lean toward multi-ethnic/cultural inclusion with a view and a plan toward your idea of excellence. If you hold the value of excellence over and above diverse inclusion, you will risk your limited notion of "excellence" trumping inclusion too often and hindering the progress of the vision. Naturally, this requires prayer and good judgment. In fact, even better, broaden your idea of excellence to include diverse richness.

FASTING AND PRAYER

Yes, I'm writing this one twice. The evil one hates this diverse unity effort. The greatest threat to his decreasing kingdom of darkness is the united church of Jesus Christ, especially expressed in local fellowships and city/regional collectives. That's why Paul includes the spiritual armor set of instructions in Ephesians 6. In that letter, he has spent five chapters outlining the plan of God through the blood-bought diversely united church, and he concludes by telling them Satan will hate this and fight hard. Hence, put on the armor of God and pray. Fasting and prayer are essential tools and disciplines for any believer and church but are a matter of life and death for any Kingdom work intentionally leaning into being an answer to Jesus' prayer at the Last Supper: "My prayer is not for them alone. I pray also for those who will believe in me through their message, that all of them may be one, Father, just as you are in me and I am in you. May they also be in us so that the world may believe that you have sent me" (John 17:20-21).

» Teach on the power of fasting and prayer.
» Model it.
» Lead corporate opportunities along the way.

» Make specific calls to fasting and prayer days during weeks when key things are taking place.

» Have a permanent weekly corporate prayer meeting of some kind, no matter how small.

» Don't neglect or underestimate the importance of this weapon. You pay too great a price along the way—you, your family and the congregation you serve.

» Practice a weekly fasting and prayer day yourself. For me it's typically Wednesdays, from Tuesday after dinner to Wednesday dinner.

DEAL WITH UNCHECKED PATRIOTISM

Passion for your own country, its origins, nostalgia of its specialness over and above other nations is divisive and can be idolatrous. As a Caucasian American, I had to learn how my reverencing of America's founding as spiritual, exceptional, and even biblical (as if any nation other than the Jewish people, or the *ekklesia* of Jews and nations could be so), my revering of America as if it were the New Jerusalem, was idolatry rooted in my heart. I also had to learn that I could not lead the church or my own life to be rid of racism while holding up racist founders of America as heroes in my life or to our congregation. The blending of patriotism and worship is simply unbiblical, and it's divisive.

This is not easy to do if raised white and Christian in America. Nor is it easy for any nationality with unchecked or comparative pride. But it's essential heart-work to be done for any local church desirous to unite in our common identity produced through the gospel of Jesus Christ. Second Corinthians 5:17, "Therefore, if anyone is in Christ, the new creation has come: The old has gone, the new is here!" This doesn't mean that we have nothing good to celebrate in our national heritage, but let it be based on truth and humility. Without truth, we will have no reconciliation. Selective history is painful and divisive to those not benefited by our country, or worse, those sinned against. Let our most substantial history be that once we were dead in our trespasses and sins, and now we live through Christ in us, as one new humanity (Ephesians 2:1-16).

LANGUAGE SERVICES AND FELLOWSHIPS, IN-STEAD OF SEPARATE ETHNIC CONGREGATIONS

Language can be a practical barrier to a diversely united church. So can be the immigrant survival experience for first-generation internationals. To have truly shared leadership and power, every need met, every part contributing, and the whole body enriched, first-generation immigrants likely will need a subset fellowship or language service. They have magnified needs the rest of us don't have. Everyday life is a struggle to learn how to survive and thrive in a new homeland. Language is a barrier, and culture provides many, many barriers. We need to reach them with the gospel, but we should do so without total segregation, or their children or grandchildren might leave the ethnic/language church and possibly leave Christ, not discerning the difference. They may reject Christ and church, when really they would be rejecting subcultured, isolated, seemingly irrelevant-to-life-now, and segregated and siloed worship. Unwittingly, they would also lose rich heritage and generational blessing they need in their lives, richness that also blesses the multicultured, multiethnic local church when first-generation immigrants find a way to be one body with a majority language congregation.

Further, biblically speaking, John hears languages in his vision of Revelation 7:9, does he not? Or else how would he know the gathering is a multitude of peoples, nations, tribes, and *tongues*? He sees and hears their differences, yet he visions one multitude together worshiping as one.

At Peoples Church Cincinnati, we have two English services, one Spanish, and one Amharic (Ethiopians and Eritreans). The children and youth are combined. The three language services do groups, serve, lead, and give as one. We have one board and one staff. Further, the first-generation immigrants are encouraged to attend an English service as they acclimate to the church. Quarterly we have "all in" Sundays where everyone attends an enhanced English service (with songs and sermon notes translated and projected on the screen). Close to bi-monthly, we have "all in" food and fellowship events.

HOLIDAYS

Listen to one another. Consider how to celebrate special days together, especially Christmas, the New Year, and Easter, and go easy on national holidays in light of taking care not to allow nationalism to trump Kingdom. As for the universal believers' holidays of Christmas, the Resurrection, and Pentecost and traditions for how to start a new year, be sensitive to the unique expressions in the ethnic and national streams of the congregation, and creatively allow these to enrich the whole. Even if you don't combine traditions every year, and you make room for separate language and cultural celebrations, consider communicating and celebrating those traditions in the English services, and invite all to join in on all experiences.

FINDING WAYS TO DO "ALL-IN"

At times early on and along the way we sought food, fun, and fellowship opportunities that were all-in, with laughter, fun, and celebration. These days make the glue. Our Taste of Nations every late summer is a specific example. On that day, everyone brings some recipe they learned from Mom or Dad, Grandma or Granddad, and we share a food festival together with all the food tables organized in the mega-groups of the church (African American, Euro-American, Latino, Asian, East African, West African, European, etc.).

COMMON DENOMINATORS

Beyond the obvious ones, like Jesus, the gospel, the Great Commission, and the Bible as authoritative and Spirit-inspired, we've found that everyone cares about children and youth. So find ways to team together for their benefit.

» Children: As a wise Ethiopian Christian leader once shared, to invest in the children is to "redeem the time" because every child becomes an adult whose life will produce much fruit for the Kingdom. We all share that vision about our kids. And it's especially edifying when we share that vision for one another's kids.

» Marriage health: Everyone wants and needs this!

» Communion, baptism, the Holy Spirit! These are what Paul lays out at the top of Ephesians 4 right after establishing the power of the mystery of Christ now being revealed, many backgrounds, one body! With these

core ingredients as common, we have much on which to set our minds
and hearts together as one.

» At the risk of redundancy—food! Everyone loves food and loves to
share their heritage foods! Capitalize on this easy win through shared
experiences in small groups and fellowship events. Therein cultures,
stories, and lives are shared. Shared experiences create relational fusion.

Preach Multifaceted, Many-textured Sermons

This cannot be underscored enough. Not only drawing from many parts
of the Bible throughout the three-year diet of the church, but within each
message layer illustrations and humor styles. This requires preachers to grow
immensely in their repertoire. Your TV, movie, reading, and music diet has
to become variegated so that your preaching illustrations will be as well. At
the same time, recognize that you will always be somewhat limited to your
upbringing and somewhat captive to your family and culture of origin.
That said, share the pulpit! Allow the preaching to come from your diverse
staff, or diverse lay leaders, or diverse ministry friends. If you don't have any
diversity in your sphere, change that now. Then, proceed.

"Assimilation" Is a Cuss Word

In the multi-ethnic/economic church, assimilation simply ends up meaning
everyone conforms to the dominant culture or group. Prefer to embrace,
celebrate, and include diverse beauty, culture, and richness—uniting without
losing self; uniting without sacrificing flavor, color, sounds, and perspectives
that actually comprise the "manifold wisdom" being announced into the
"heavenly realms" (Ephesians 3:10). So have inclusion processes but not
assimilation. At Peoples, we have a five-step Inclusion experience for our
Growth Track.

Make the Complex Simple, Understandable, and Scalable without Losing Richness

At the risk of redundancy, I'm going to share a few more thoughts on how
to think about diverse unity in your how-you-do-church strategy. Here I'm
primarily talking about ideas, systems, processes, and values. Often for the

sake of efficiency and scalability, we sacrifice the texture, the cultural richness, the flavors, and the depth needed to hold multiple groups in an inclusive mix. That can be death to diverse unity and usually leads to assimilation to the dominant culture. And as we just said, don't cuss.

Simplifying without sacrificing is a skill you can grow. We're still learning it at Peoples Church and Network and are getting better at it as we go; so will you. And here's a key, don't do this alone! Don't do any of this alone. A quote by Ken Blanchard reads like this, "NONE OF US is as smart as ALL OF US." As your team/staff, volunteer and paid, grows in depth and knowledge and insight for church-as-heaven-on-earth, the energy of collaborative problem-solving will allow the church to figure out simplifying the complex without compromising richness. As you teach, use multiple words for the same thing. In doing so, you can in a few words feed minds from the more educated to the less, from the more English fluent to the first-generation immigrant, from the south to the north. For example, you might use the word "fecundity" followed by "fruitfulness" in the same sentence, inspiring the educated and translating for the less so. Fast use of diverse language allows you to hold a multi-economic, multi-educated, multi-generational, multicultural congregation together for His glory!

Keyboard-based Worship

Early on, we learned that nothing helps more to diversify our worship experience for everyone than having different skin tones on stage. We also realized we needed diversity of sounds and rhythms, syncopations and moods within our music to speak to the growing cultural complexity of our congregation. With guitar-led-only contemporary Christian music we were not going to hold very many people of color, or those of southern hemisphere upbringings, for very long. Feeling the music, and feeling the passion of the leaders was also paramount for so many of our people to worship with their whole being—body, mind, and soul. Euro-descent worshipers could get along with the "white" feel of CCM and guitar-based experiences, but a mix of soulful, gospel, multicultural sounds and keyboard-based worship would also be necessary. When the Lord gave us that, through the life of a young, white man raised in the church, we were off to the races for greater inclusion.

Jason Sharp began leading toward the end of 2002, from a piano that he played with gospel rhythms and sounds. He introduced Israel Houghton, Kirk Franklin, and Donnie McClurkin and international multicultural sounds to worship for our body. I'll never forget how the few people of color in the church rushed me after his first service and celebrated with me that *now* they felt the worship. I also won't forget the visit to my office by two older pillars in the church letting me know they and their wives weren't too pleased with our new direction. I listened, I loved on these men, and I thanked them for their concern. Then I shared why the change was so necessary. One of them is still living and actively serves as an usher in our early service. God helped him and his wife see and celebrate the bigger purposes beyond personal preference.

TRADITIONS

Keep some and make new ones as the body grows diversely. The ones you keep, translate them into the new reality of the church. The new ones will become precious and provide cohesion for everyone. An old one we have kept is our June church-wide cookout. In our new reality today, the foods and the fun are a celebration of the diverse richness of our church. The softball game has given way to soccer, and the desserts are now from all over the world, the deep South (peach cobbler!), and from Cincinnati's German heritage as well! A new tradition is our Christmas Day service and meal. Never in a million years did I believe the American part of our church would buy into this expected and cherished celebration by the international part of our body, but year by year we see young American families, single adults, and older couples joining in with the international body. Traditions create shared experiences and cohesion, ethnically, culturally, and generationally.

DENOMINATIONAL BACKGROUNDS MIXING

As you grow multiculturally, so will your denominational backgrounds increase. With that can come precious contributions but also tricky disagreements. As in everything, let Scripture help you. I find Ephesians 4:1-6 to be apropos and essential. So, maximize the opportunities and minimize the obstacles.

PARENTING NEW CHURCHES AND CAMPUSES

Let good theology, ecclesiology, and missiology be your guide. Don't give in to homogeneous church planting. If you plant, and the result is a one-culture haven despite all your efforts, keep coaching, encouraging, teaching, guiding, and praying with your leaders. Give them all the support and help you can possibly afford. Pray and stay steady. Further, make a strategic and budgetary priority to multiply churches-like-heaven-on-earth. More disciples will be made. More Kingdom increase will come to every community where you and your teams plant gospel-centered Ephesians 2:15 and John 17:21 churches.

ABOVE-TITHE GIVING

We recommend one-above-tithe bucket for simplicity and scale. We use the idea of ACCESS giving. We create ACCESS for all people to the King and His Kingdom through three methods: (1) missions: supporting and sending boots-on-the-ground missionaries to and toward unreached people groups (see Joshua Project List, joshuaproject.net); (2) biblical justice (fatherless, immigrants, widows, the poor); (3) church multiplication. One bucket, ACCESS, feeds these three streams. Each November, we vision-cast for the coming year and people make one-year goals, above tithes. It works, and we have fuel to create access for all people to the King and His Kingdom in our city, the nation, and among unreached people groups (UPGs) around the earth.

MISSIONS AND JUSTICE—A CLOSER LOOK

For many white evangelical churches, the idea of international missions is essential. The Great Commission calls for taking the gospel to every ethnos (people group). What might be difficult for some white evangelicals—as it was for me at first—is to understand how equally essential to the spread of the gospel is biblical justice. Isaiah 58 (God-desired fasting leads to light breaking forth) actually ties them together and so does James 1:27 (pure religion), and 1 John 3:23 (being in the truth involves belief in Christ and love), and we can easily make the case right from Matthew 28:20, "teaching them to obey everything I have commanded." For some black evangelicals and anyone who might suggest (because of all the work to be done here in the United States) we have no good reason to send ministry and dollars overseas, one has to come to grips with the Matthew 24:14 (gospel of the Kingdom must be proclaimed in all the earth, to every people, before the end will come), Matthew 28:18-20 (disciples of all *ethne*, every people group) and the geographic outward movement of Acts 1:8 (Jerusalem, Judea, Samaria, and to the uttermost parts of the earth).

At Peoples Church, our solution to this false dichotomy has been to create an unashamed inclusion of both missions and biblical justice priorities within our ministry philosophy, initiatives, and our above-tithe giving vehicle called ACCESS, mentioned above. The vision is to help create access for all people to Jesus and His Kingdom through evangelism *and* justice work. So our ACCESS giving goes into three categories: unreached people group missions, biblical justice, and church/vision multiplication. Our intentional interest and strategic actions are to look for these three threads in every ministry we support financially and also to engage these three priorities locally and globally through active prayer and Kingdom building efforts as a local church.

MISSIONS TEAM

A lay team of missions-informed and passionate people oversee the ACCESS UPG dollars and lift the priority of UPGs for the whole congregation. They meet monthly and are doing great work.

JUSTICE TEAM

This is a motivated team of high-capacity folk who steward and lead the biblical and racial justice energy and initiatives of the church and help steward the ACCESS justice dollars.

PEOPLES CHURCH NETWORK ELDERS

This group oversees the ACCESS Multiply dollars from each of our churches and the vision of multiplying church-like-heaven-on-earth.

STRATEGIC PLANNING

God has placed many gifts in every local church. Let each part do its work. As pastors allow marketplace leaders to share the load, assisting with infrastructure, operations, and strategic planning of the church's future, the Kingdom experiences increase. (See FOCUS Game by Dave Workman.)

STRATEGIC PARTNERSHIPS: LOCAL

In order to facilitate local engagement in evangelism, discipleship, and biblical justice work, we've found we don't have to invent everything by ourselves. The guiding principle here is that the whole church ministering the whole gospel to the whole city can accomplish so much more than we can as individual congregations disconnected from each other.

That's not to say there aren't any initiatives we do on our own. We do. But when it comes to the bigger things, we work with partners for maximizing impact. And on all the smaller initiatives, we cheer one another other on and celebrate the wins as a team-win for all: Greater Cincy Urban Young Life, CityLink Center, *Undivided*, Race to Unity, Mosaix Cincy Network, Whole Again, City Gospel Mission, Coalition of Care, Beacon of Hope Business Alliance, Cru (Campus Crusade), City Servants, Unify Cincy, Outpouring, Declare Cincinnati, and many gospel-centered local church partnerships across denominational and racial lines.

STRATEGIC PARTNERSHIPS: STATE AND NATIONAL

In the same way, for national impact work we find and cooperate with like-hearted national or statewide networks—whether in the multi-ethnic church movement, like with Mosaix Global Network, or for biblical justice or church multiplication. For church multiplication, we network with Acts 29, Stadia, CMN, OCMN, ARC, etc. In the area of biblical justice, we synergize with Backyard Orphan, Ohio Justice and Policy Center, AMOS Project, John M. Perkins Foundation, CCDA, and many others.

STRATEGIC PARTNERSHIPS: INTERNATIONAL

LiveDead (website), Wycliffe, Athletes in Action, AGWM, Prayer Covenant for Kids, OneHope, Convoy of Hope, Cru, Project 42, Joshua Project.

STORIES OF SPIRITUAL WAR

All along the way we've learned and experienced many times over: The real fight happens in the spiritual realm. This spiritual struggle, as Ephesians 6 points out, is not to be taken lightly. It's real. It can be ferocious. But it does not need to be feared. We are equipped for it, or we can be, if we let the

Word of God be the guide to our methods. Paul says to armor up and be a person of much prayer. We learned this to be so true during our nearly two decades' journey in this vision. Let me share a few stories:

One Saturday service some years ago, we were excited to share our newly created Psalm 23 video. The ninety-second clip was set to go during the worship portion of the service. As it played, the audience would hear Psalm 23 quoted on screen by different Peoples Church folk in their native languages. It opened with a middle-aged white American woman and ended with a young African American man, Terry Thomas, with several other beautiful languages of the world in between, subscripted in English. The audience was soaking in this powerful experience. As the video began to roll, a massive bolt of lightning struck our building, blowing out all the power—a literal bolt of lightning struck our building. Simultaneously our children's ministry spaces began to flood! Clearly, from my view anyway, the prince of the air was unhappy with the power of this video and its testimony of harmonized, diverse lives as one body, publicly quoting the Word of God as one.

The hilarious and beautiful part of the whole experience was when our worship band, which was standing ready to play lightly at the end of the video, picked up a melody acoustically. Before long the vocalists joined in, and the service just kept rolling. It was so impactful, revealing a live experience of real-time opposition that did not throw the church off its assignment: to bring Him united worship and declare the "manifold wisdom of God" into the heavenlies (Ephesians 3:9-10). I knew from that very moment that this video threatened darkness. More significantly, what we were all about as a church was rocking hell. I like to show that clip and tell this story whenever I speak on Revelation 5:9-10.

Here's another story. In 2018, as many new ministry initiatives and leaders had been emerging, we entered a month of crazy. Two of our leaders were accused of egregious sin, two received death threats, one leadership couple's marriage imploded, a deacon suffered a house fire, another the loss of a four-year-old niece in a car accident. Painful, disorienting, and like taking on a meteor shower of spiritual attacks, we were jolted. Jan and I set aside many days to fast and pray. We spent hours sorting through the situations. All along the way, we understood our "struggle is not against flesh and blood, but against the rulers, against the authorities, against the powers of this dark world and against the spiritual forces of evil in the heavenly [spiritual] realms" (Ephesians 6:12). But we were still rocked to our core.

We don't pretend to fully understand this Kingdom fight. But we know it's real, and we know our weapons for the fight are spiritual, not fleshly. That said, these battles take a toll and, for sure, can burn a lot of energy. So we try to stay vigilant, prayerful, rested, united, and faithful, practicing the armor truths and principles listed in Ephesians 6. When you consider that Paul includes spiritual battle instruction at the end of one of his premier diverse/unity books, Ephesians, it underscores how much the evil one must hate the work of one-new-humanity church. On the other side of these months of crazy, our team has come out stronger and more united than ever.

(Some of the previous paragraph was written Friday, July 6, 2018, shortly after noon.) Within two hours of typing that last sentence, hell unleashed a massive torpedo into the side of our ship. There's more to this part of the story, and it involves an email interaction with N. T. Wright between the time of finishing those last words and a tornadic spiritual attack. I'll cut and paste that thread into here for illustration of how spiritual war can work. For context, I will include the beginning of our interaction all the way back to 2017.

> From: chris@peopleschurch.co
> Date: September 21, 2017 at 6:38:02 AM EDT
> To: N. T. Wright
> Subject: Ephesians 2:15, Golf (Cincinnati) :)
> Dr. Wright,
>
> For some months I've been intending to follow up after your Cincinnati visit.
>
> At the morning leaders gathering someone raised a question about race. I followed with a thought from Ephesians 2, and you responded that you appreciated the topic being 'teed up' like when your golf instructor does at your lesson.

Afterward I asked if you'd considered the Acts 20 Ephesian Elders meeting and Paul's statement 'the whole plan/will of God' in light of Ephesians 1, 2, 3.

Since last spring I've been prayerfully reflecting on this as the 'strategic plan' of God to 'bring all things under His feet.'

In short, I believe the Church needs a theology/ecclesiology/missiology of church as heaven on earth, one new humanity, a diversely united blood bought bride of every tribe, tongue and people, experiencing and exhibiting John 17:20-23.

I don't know if this has yet been written (excepting the letter to the Ephesians :), and from deep in my heart I believe the Lord is prompting me to work on this.

Could we talk sometime, even for just 20 minutes? Or, could I send you a short article I've drafted so far entitled, The Ephesian Elders Meeting?

–Chris

From: chris@peopleschurch.co [mailto:chris@peopleschurch.co]
Sent: 29 September 2017 15:58
To: Tom N.T. Wright
Subject: Fwd: Ephesians 2:14 and a teed up golf ball (in Cincinnati)

Good day sir, I continue to feel impressed of the Lord to connect with you about Acts 20 and Ephesians 2.

I pastor an 110 year old Assemblies of God church in Cincinnati. I've been on staff 25 years.

In a month I'll be at Fuller Seminary (Amos Yong is a friend) sharing our church experience in their Race and Missiology confab. I've also shared about it at Wheaton College (Inhabit Conference 2014).

I only mention these things to show this is not a passing fancy for me, but a deep biblical conviction that seems to have prophetic traction for the Church (academia and practitioners alike) in the earth at this hour, as I think you are well aware.

Please see brief thoughts below...

My ask of you is simply a 20-minute phone call for guidance. And I'll be so grateful even for 10, realizing the crushing demands on your time.

Is it possible for me to get on your schedule? If so, how?

–Chris

On Sep 29, 2017, at 11:45 AM, Tom N.T. Wright wrote:

Hi Chris, thanks for this.

At the moment I am scrambling every hour of every day to keep up. September–October is my busy-busy classroom time and the minute that's over I head (this year) to Wheaton for a week of lectures etc., then back to be with my postgrads (and my family!). I am struggling to draft the outline for the Gifford Lectures for next spring in Aberdeen. Can you possibly send me a paragraph or two with your basic question/idea and I'll see if I can respond quickly?

Best wishes

–Tom Wright

After a multi-month delay in correspondence with Wright, I felt prompted in my spirit to reach out to him once more—just to seek validation that my definitive position in this book wasn't off. This time, as I went back to reread his most recent email, I noticed his question from September 29, 2017, which I had missed responding to at that time—namely, "Can you possibly send me a paragraph or two with your basic question/idea and I'll see if I can respond quickly?" Following is continued correspondence starting July 2018.

From: chris@peopleschurch.co [mailto:chris@peopleschurch.co]
Sent: 06 July 2018 17:57
To: Tom N.T. Wright
Subject: Re: Ephesians 2:14-16 and a teed up golf ball (in Cincinnati, 2017)

Hi Tom,

Some time has passed since our brief email interchange below . . .

For the past 6 months I've been working on these thoughts in a book format, Ephesus: Jesus' Diversely-United, Blood-purchased Church.

In your initial response below you asked for my question. I think it's this . . . do you think there's an insight, an apologetic for the Gospel we're missing because of the richness-limited witness our segregated, homogeneous congregations?

And follow up...are we also thereby inadvertently missing the strategic plan of God?

Discussing this with you for even a few moments is what was on my heart, but I also welcome a written response of any kind.

I wouldn't bother you with this if I didn't continue to feel in prayer that this may be a big deal for us as the Church and that the simple theology and reality of church-like-heaven-on-earth (multi-tribe, diversely united congregations) and its implications needs to get out to church leaders in the earth.

For a glimpse of the thoughts I've been having on this I'm attaching my article, The Ephesian Model, just published in the Assemblies of God USA clergy magazine, Influence.

Thankful for you and your thought leadership for the Church.
–Chris

On Jul 6, 2018, at 1:15 PM, Tom N.T. Wright wrote:

Dear Chris
Thanks for this and apologies that I am still horribly busy, chasing all sorts of projects and deadlines near and far. The answers to your questions are YES and YES. And there's much more I could say but just to encourage you: all this is spot on to what I think Paul would say to our churches today (Have you seen my Biography of Paul?)
Warm greetings
–Tom

On Jul 6, 2018, at 1:51 PM, chris@peopleschurch.co wrote:

FANTASTIC, Tom! That helps fuel me forward. I'll check out your Paul biography.
–Chris

From: chris@peopleschurch.co [mailto:chris@peopleschurch.co]
Sent: 13 July 2018 19:20
To: Tom N.T. Wright
Subject: Re: Ephesians 2:14-16 and a teed up golf ball (in Cincinnati, 2017)
Tom,
Within 30 minutes of my sending you this response (below) last Friday . . . an email blast with an accusation against one of our ethnic minority staff pastors went out to the leadership of the church, and by the next day to many members of the body . . . Ephesians 6 has never been so real to me.
–Chris

Date: July 14, 2018 at 12:53:02 PM EDT
To: chris@peopleschurch.co
Subject: RE: Ephesians 2:14-16 and a teed up golf ball (in Cincinnati, 2017)

I am not surprised . . .
Best wishes
–Tom

Can you believe that blow at that moment, just minutes removed from an email exchange of validation of these theological observations? I wouldn't have either, but what a blow! It took me away from writing for nine weeks. After making it through the teeth of the storm, we gently pulled the ship into harbor for repairs and safety checks, having sustained some of the worst blows of our ministry life. I wish I could say we had no damage, but many injuries were sustained, many hours consumed, and much energy expended.

At the same time, God is sovereign, and His purposes, plans, and protection continue to prevail. Our team is wiser, more deeply united, and more experienced as a diversely included eldership of lay and pastoral leaders, and more dependent on the Lord and one another than ever. We took a couple of months to recover, but soon we were sensing His favor to press forward. For example: (1) One of our new Peoples Network churches that launched in the spring of 2018 hit 107 in attendance on Easter Sunday a year later, and by then had already celebrated their first six baptisms. (2) In 2018, our Network's founding campus, uptown in Cincinnati, hosted a national meeting of leaders focused on *receiving* from African American pastors in the American church as well as an emphasis on diverse inclusion as an ultimate strategy of the Kingdom. (3) Also in 2018, we cosponsored a gospel-centered educational event at Cincinnati Christian University, *Race 2 Unity*, which pulls up roots of racism and racial separation in evangelical Christianity by inviting audiences to examine heart matters around race, history, nationalism, and the church of Jesus Christ in America. Meanwhile our Cincinnati Uptown campus flourished after this attack and despite recently hiving off sixty leaders in the spring of 2018 to launch Peoples

East Cincinnati, just one year after opening Peoples Church St. Louis, each Peoples Church congregation is vibrant and accelerating, to His glory.

Theologically, I've come to believe that psalms like Psalm 83 speak to the way the enemy works against his worst fears, the successes of the people of God that threaten darkness:

> See how your enemies growl, how your foes rear their heads. With cunning they conspire against your people; they plot against those you cherish. "Come," they say, "let us destroy them as a nation, so that Israel's name is remembered no more." With one mind they plot together; they form an alliance against you—the tents of Edom and the Ishmaelites, of Moab and the Hagrites, Byblos, Ammon and Amalek, Philistia, with the people of Tyre. Even Assyria has joined them to reinforce Lot's descendants. (Psalm 83:2-8)

This psalm references the conspiring of multiple enemies of God's people. What I believe that might mean in the spiritual realm for us in the New Covenant era is that when darkness is under threat by the Kingdom of God, and the work of the people of God through Christ in them, the enemy fights harder, smarter, more conspiringly, utilizing multiple "forces of evil in [spiritual] realms." In other words, the fight becomes more fierce and more complex at times. Ephesians 6:12 warns that our battle is not against one another or in the natural world but in the spiritual realms. So the application of the full armor and weaponry of Ephesians 6 is essential, in light of how the enemy will sometimes battle against us.

One more crucial scriptural connection in this area is Isaiah 59, one of the more soaring justice passages in the Bible. There we find expressions like, "No one calls for justice; no one pleads a case with integrity. They rely on empty arguments, they utter lies; they conceive trouble and give birth to evil" and "So justice is far from us, and righteousness does not reach us. We look for light, but all is darkness; for brightness, but we walk in deep shadows" (59:9) and "So justice is driven back, and righteousness stands at a distance; truth has stumbled in the streets, honesty cannot enter" (59:14).

Seeing no one to intervene, Isaiah was appalled; "so his own arm achieved salvation for him, and his own righteousness sustained him. He put on *righteousness as his breastplate, and the helmet of salvation* on his head; he put on the garments of vengeance and wrapped himself in zeal as in a cloak" (Isaiah 59:16-17, italics mine). "Stand firm then, with the belt of truth buckled around your waist, with the breastplate of righteousness in place. . . . Take the helmet of salvation and the sword of the Spirit, which is the word of God" (Ephesians 6:14, 17). I'm not even exactly sure what to make of this parallel between Isaiah 59 and Ephesians 6, except to say that walking out biblical justice will be fought hard by authorities in dark places, and from Isaiah to Paul is an understanding of how to prepare for the fight. We have to prepare.

I share these stories so you, too, will be awake and aware, that 2 Peter 1:5-9 will be a sword in your hand, and so you will know it's not your fault when the onslaught begins. In fact, expect a level of war when pushing Kingdom things forward. Steel yourself. Don't shrink back. "But we do not belong to those who shrink back and are destroyed, but to those who have faith and are saved" (Hebrews 10:39). "They triumphed over him by the blood of the Lamb and by the word of their testimony; they did not love their lives so much as to shrink from death" (Revelation 12:11). Profound, spine-stiffening stuff.

NONNEGOTIABLES

» Good theology
» Good ecclesiology
» Good missiology
» Good theology of gospel-centered justice
» Diversely united leadership, in everything (If you don't have it, don't rest until you do.)
» Fasting and prayer
» Healthy personal walk in Christ
» Multiply (vision, disciples, leaders, churches, networks)

PEOPLES CHURCH NETWORK FOR CHURCH MULTIPLICATION

A network eldership was formed in 2018 out of the three founding Peoples Network churches in Cincinnati and St. Louis to steward the theology, culture, and church multiplication vision and dollars. (See PCN website at peopleschurch.co.)

PRAXIS—CHURCH COLLECTIVE

Chapter 55

LOCAL IMPACT

At this very writing I just came off an amazing day of watching God at work through the diverse church collective in Cincinnati.

Our mayor and city manager, one white and one black, are at a fractious crossroads. Neither has a personal walk with Jesus as far as I can yet tell, but they are talented men who have led well despite making their share of mistakes. This week however, in early 2018, they are in a messy and public feud that portends to exacerbate our city's racial divide. City council is at a loss as to what to do. The talk radio, black and white (yes, we have functionally segregated radio talk shows, of which most whites in our city are entirely unaware, as was I for many years), are aflame with vitriol.

So where will the solution come from?

During a meeting of city Kingdom leaders yesterday, after a time of corporate prayer, the Holy Spirit prompted one from our pastors who said, "A team of clergy needs to go to city hall and speak life over this situation." Within a few hours a meeting for the next morning was set up with the mayor and city manager.

The outcomes are still to be determined, but here's what happened today: five pastors, both white and black, from five different denominational affiliations met at city hall for prayer together. Then we met with the estranged mayor and city manager. Our words were few: We've come to pray with you. No media. No discussions. Just prayer over your lives in the name of Jesus Christ, the King of kings, and to implore the Father for wisdom to reign in your lives, over this situation, and over our city.

These two leaders agreed. They agreed because they already know us. They know that our friendships and respect for one another are deep. They have also experienced our love toward each of them during other crisis moments in the life of the city. But now, it was about them.

We shared our words; we prayed. We didn't even sit down. We stood in a circle, finished, hugged them, and walked out. They remained alone to work on the matter together.

The staff in the outer offices were stunned and smiling. Palpable tension was gripping the air before we went in, the same as it has been over the whole city. And it may soon return to that office—we don't know.

But here's what we do know: A diversely united church of Jesus Christ carries a humble spiritual authority that can speak into human affairs.

How did we get this opportunity?

This story is one that speaks to the power of the diverse church united in a community, a robust church willing to work on the deep matters, whatever they may be, through our common bond in the Lord Jesus and His Kingdom principles and through genuine love for one another and concern for one another's burdens.

I've already written about some of the collective Kingdom experiences and efforts we're enjoying so far in Cincinnati, in large part due to the diverse unity in the body through Christ and His gospel (Race to Unity, City Servants).

Through the years, many more life-giving initiatives have emerged for our city. Let me share a few more.

CityLink Center, City Gospel Mission, The Healing Center. In the late 1990s, a unique group of parachurch leaders in the urban core began to meet together for regular prayer. As they did, common vision for holistic ministry among the poor of our city emerged. Before long, personal and organizational agendas were being mutually submitted to the greater good of cooperative, collective impact.

What if some of our ministries merged under the same roof or administration to reduce costs or create a "one-stop shop" for people in need of services? One of the great challenges for the poor is transportation. When multiple ministry and agency locations are spread across a city or a county, the transportation challenges burn significant amounts of energy and limited financial resources. One place might assist with housing solutions, another with GED completion, and still another with job readiness programs. As these humble parachurch Christian leaders began to pray together and ask, "What if?" God moved on hearts to simplify, converge, and scale their best practice efforts. Over time, several key expressions of wraparound supports emerged: CityLink Center, a reimagined City Gospel Mission, and The Healing Center.

Today, the working poor, the formerly incarcerated, the recent immigrant or refugee, the formerly addicted are all able to receive an ally in Christ, and experience a thoughtful, thorough, dignifying process toward wholeness and sustainable life-health. I don't believe any of these powerful concepts now realized would exist without those early uniting prayer meetings, cross-racial and cross-denominational, and at potential cost to self. The church united is impactful.

Whole Again. Before experiencing racially and economically inclusive church, I discovered life realities I never knew about the urban core and communities of poverty. One such reality is that during summer break from school, many children go without meals every day. During the school year, they would receive free/reduced school breakfast and lunch. A godly church leader of color in our city decided to do something about it.

Pastor Greg Chandler rallied lay leaders from evangelical churches of all hues and diverse dogma to cooperate smartly against this challenge. Whole Again was born. Now for ten weeks every summer, thousands of Cincinnati children attend church-based day programs and receive two nutritious meals daily and a take-home bag for the weekend. That's collective impact. Pastor Greg and I go back many years as we've enjoyed two decades of friendship through our intentionally cross-racial, pastors' covenant group. I still remember our drive together along the Jordan River valley in the Palestinian West Bank with another mutual friend, Troy Jackson, dreaming the dream together of scaling African American–led, game-changing initiatives for Cincinnati. Greg, a man of action and vision, led us forward.

Outpouring. In a city servants (discussed earlier) leadership meeting one day, Troy Jackson lifted a compelling vision. What if we held a corporate worship and prayers service and invited proven, influential, and godly leaders from across the region, lifting the name of Jesus and using Scripture to pray into the leading indicators of Cincinnati's brokenness.

Recently we'd learned of our top five national ranking among similar-sized cities for child poverty. This stunning fact would provide the motivation for a clarion call. And Outpouring was born. We would select a large venue for Pentecost Sunday afternoon and jointly, unitedly elevate the name of Jesus and the needs of our city in prayer. Before long, a richly diverse planning team was formed including Catholics and Protestants; black, brown, white; female and male; evangelicals and progressives; believing Jews and Gentiles. That service gathered only a little over a thousand believers, but the collection was so richly diverse and so humbly united that as different respected leaders prayed through Isaiah 65, the room was electric.

Something shifted in the heavens over our city that year (Ephesians 3:10). We're enjoying increasingly deeper unity and cooperation for big tasks year by year, moving the needle of health and life for all people in our city. We have a very long way to go, but recognizable mutuality and shared effort are increasing. And Jesus' name is getting the glory.

Mosaix Cincy Network. In the mid-2000s, our executive pastor, Brandon Wilkes (now pastoring Peoples Church St. Louis) entered my office to lay a magazine on my desk in front of me. "Chris, this article sounds just like you." I lifted the copy to see a picture of Mark DeYmaz and his words about multi-ethnic church. As I read the *Ministry Today* article, I was floored. Brandon was right; we were saying and experiencing many of the same things as Mark and Mosaic Church in Little Rock, Arkansas.

Before long Mark and I were sharing hearts over the phone and joining together in like-minded fashion for the work of our King. A few years later, our whole pastoral team attended the 2010 Mosaix Global Network national conference and for the first time were surrounded by other intentionally multi-ethnic ministries. Mark, George Yancey, and Mosaix had been at work for many years to gather leaders and resources for mutual encouragement and benefit toward the task of a living church-like-heaven-on-earth.

One direct outcome for me was that we needed to start a local area common table in Cincinnati. Along came Marc Champagne with just such a vision. Marc was preparing to plant Redeemer Church in the north of our city and wondered who else might be out there thinking intentionally and theologically about doing diversely united church. Initially, we were just three white guys, one of whom soon dropped out. But before long the table grew. We had to go from meeting over lunch in different ethnic food restaurants around the city to a more predictable, permanent location. Marc suggested our space at Peoples. We also realized the strength in starting this as a city cohort/network under the Mosaix umbrella for name recognition, scaling, and national cooperation.

What a great decision these steps turned out to be. Soon our group was averaging thirty-five leaders from about eighty different regularly involved churches and ministries, all at different spots along the spectrum of growth toward Revelation 5:9 church. To our surprise and joy, many historic and new, small and large, diverse-background, gospel-centered churches joined in.

The lead team soon realized the additional benefit of a triennial *regional* Mosaix Global Network conference in Cincinnati. These meetings ballooned into the hundreds, well beyond our initial expectations and hopes of a hundred attendees. Under the masterful guidance of Oneya Okuwobi, Sherman Bradley, and Tom Baxter, these regional meetings pumped vision, life, and practical tools into many of Cincinnati's most motivated gospel-rooted churches. Church reflecting heaven on earth is growing in our region, and we're approaching critical mass.

Undivided. Our relationship with Crossroads Church goes back to the beginning. One of the founding couples, Brian and Nancy Wells, was leading the young adult ministry at our church in the early to mid-1990s when the Lord spoke to their hearts to plant a new church along with their friends from three other life-giving churches across the city. Each contributing church pastor gave their blessing to this core group of eleven who had a dream.

The new church exploded onto the scene with an unusual level of momentum and energy under the apt leadership of Brian and Libby Tome. God had sent them to our city. Early on, Brian Tome invited me to serve with him and the founding eldership in a friendship "advisory board" capacity. What fun that was those first three years as the church soared. After three years, an eldership/director team from within Crossroads was in place, and my involvement could transition to the cheering section. Along the way and through the years, Tome, Wells, and I have continued to share profound conversations around race, the church of Jesus Christ, and His Kingdom.

How excited I felt to learn when Chuck Mingo, an extraordinary leader/teacher and a man of color, joined the Crossroads teaching team. Today, Chuck also serves as the site pastor for the original Oakley campus, and Crossroads multiplies across the nation under the board of directors' and Brian Tome's able leadership. Over the years, a friendship with Chuck has also developed. What a godly man and gifted leader.

I fondly remember his meeting with Jerry Culbreth and me, co-chairs of city servants Cincinnati, and asking for prayer as he was feeling called to help lead racial reconciliation in our city and beyond. Through a Crossroads small group experience and sermon series titled "Brave," God was directing him to step up and step out, first with his own race story, and then with whatever the Holy Spirit would lead. And *Undivided* was born—an experiential six-week small group course jointly developed by Crossroads with a few other church leaders focused on breaking down racial walls. In June 2018, *USA Today* front page spotlighted this amazing tool to the entire nation. This is another example of church collective, and African American–led transformation through the gospel of Jesus Christ not only flipping our city but now introduced as a tool for the whole country.

Justice Teams. One of our interfaith organizations in the city working on the common good, AMOS Project, has often been led by Christ-following evangelicals. Though its work is Good News oriented, it's not a specifically Christian organization but an interfaith one. That said, many of the Christ followers involved see their participation as Matthew 5:13-16 engagement, as "salt and light" evidence of the Kingdom of God in us. Several of our Cincinnati area churches, some because of a natural outflow from taking the *Undivided* course and some simply as an expression of their core values, which already include biblical justice, have developed Justice Teams that work on matters of racial and people justice, "societal righteousness issues" one might say (Isaiah 58–61), because of the gospel of the Kingdom in us.

In 2018, the collective work focused on public policy change that would improve tens of thousands of lives, reclassifying nonviolent, low-level drug possession felonies to misdemeanors. Not only would policy change like this save millions of tax dollars, but it would dramatically change the fatherlessness and poverty rates of so many children across Ohio's major cities and eighty-eight counties. The new law, if passed, would be retroactive, and quality of life without compromising community safety would be markedly improved.

Think about your city or state. Imagine Christ followers working in His name to directly and practically break "yokes" that keep people unemployed even after they've paid their debt to society. This would leverage the resources toward addiction treatment instead of incarceration. As a result of racially reconciling together and seeing the world through lenses we didn't have before, we're collectively and strategically working to see the common good of all lives bettered—all because of Christ in us. People far from Jesus want to consider a gospel that compels this kind of life-fruit out of Jesus' followers. And our churches are growing with economically, ethnically, and politically diverse new believers as a result. The foot of the Cross has room for all people.

Inspire Unity events. Another of the choice joys associated with what the Lord is doing in our city through His church collective is the number of marketplace (lay) leaders catalyzing Kingdom increase and enhanced momentum. Kingsley Wientge comes to mind. This local business owner has intentionally and humbly positioned himself at most of the tables and efforts described above. And Kingsley, a careful man of prayer and insight, not being one to miss a strategic God-revealed opportunity, has found a creative way to pull a number of these streams together. He's a connector, a uniter. And life in Cincinnati is better because of believing marketplace men and women like him.

Twice now, this Euro-descent man has provided an evening experience called *Inspire Unity* with live jazz music and delightful dining. This evening publicly recognizes effective local African American–owned and –led orga-nizations or initiatives that produce game-changing results through best practices. As a white, male, evangelical Christian person of means, Kingsley has taken onto himself personally the work of Matthew 5:16, "Let your light shine before others, that they may see your good deeds and glorify your Father in heaven." But not only is that the effect of his witness in the marketplace, but with a humble intensity he practices Ephesians 4:2-7, which is engendering Ephesians 4:13 unity and the resulting effect of a "fullness of Christ" in the Body, and in our city. Talk about cross-racial giving of life! The water level of the Holy Spirit is on the rise in our city, to borrow a phrase from a mid-1990s Colorado Springs leader who at the time presciently understood the power of citywide churches walking in mutual blessing toward one another under Christ (*Primary Purpose* by Ted Haggard).

Coalition of Care. I briefly mentioned the genesis of this ministry in chapter 18, but I'd like to give it a little more attention. You'll recall that during our transition from a homogeneous suburban white toward an Ephesians 2:15 church, God stirred an awakening in us regarding His heart for the orphan, a James 1:27–type revolution for us. Today this has grown into a collective church movement that portends to radically affect the foster care crisis in southwest Ohio and northern Kentucky. Through the capable leadership of Chris Combs and his diverse board of talented gospel proclaimers, Coalition of Care is discovering the secret sauce to rescue vulnerable kids through a dozen or more evidence-based, best-practice vehicles. From CarePortal to Wendy's Wonderful Kids, from Backyard Orphans church mobilization training to Safe Families, Cincinnati Coalition of Care is a fast-growing, "true religion" church collective success story.

We long for the day and believe we can see it on a ten- or twenty-year horizon when every vulnerable child and family and every exhausted social worker or foster agency leader of our city has loving wraparound support. What unimaginable pleasure this will bring to the Father, not to mention the massive number of generational brokenness cycles that will be crushed. The church diversely united through Christ ministering "religion that our Father accepts" while also walking unpolluted by the world (James 1:27) will be *shouting* the gospel with our actions. We can't wait to see the harvest of souls from this godly tsunami that is already triggered deep below the sea.

Beacon of Hope Business Alliance. What if your city or region had a business alliance of employers focused on purpose as much as profit? It might look like the Beacon of Hope birthed through the heart and humble vision of a godly Catholic brother and his team at Nehemiah Manufacturing of Cincinnati. This story was briefly shared earlier in chapter 38, but let me add that as of this writing over fifty businesses have signed onto the alliance. They're joined by the likes of CityLink, Urban League, City Gospel Mission, Jobs Plus, Cincinnati Works, Community Action Agency, and other leading local organizations whose best-practice, life-skill programs provide for the pipeline of second-chance employees. These people need work in order to provide for their families, but, historically, they have stayed unemployed or have been re-incarcerated because they re-offend out of survival or out of hopelessness. Hence the name, Beacon of Hope. Now they are proving to be the most loyal of employees; in addition, turnover rates and associated costs are measurably down for the participating businesses, and on average ten lives connected to each BoH employee experience an exciting quality-of-life shift. Here marketplace believers and the church collectively utilize their talents to accomplish Isaiah 65–type change in our city.

We believe that not only do we have an increase of Jesus followership because of the increasing diverse unity in His body across our region, but the effects of His Kingdom are benefitting generations and healing racial fractures of our history. Why? Because every one of these areas of attention have, for decades, disproportionately affected people of color in our highly racialized society. That's changing now, through racially and denomination-ally reconciling church life, marketplace engagement by the same, and no one worrying about who gets the credit. If we can bless one another and our city without needing recognition or credit, the Lord can use us for His good purposes to the same degree, without the sideways energy expense so often associated with jealousy, competition, isolationism, and apathy.

Urban Young Life, Greater Cincinnati. By the early 2000s, we were praying as local churches for Cincinnati's urban high schools. Could we have a campus ministry strategy, contextually smart and effective, with poverty-riddled urban high school students? No ministry seemed able to crack that code. Multiple times I shared about this struggle from the pulpit. One summer while on vacation, I received a call from a young leader in the church.

Normally I allow vacation calls to go to voicemail to handle later, but this call caught my attention due to the surprise reach-out by this young man. "Chris, you know how you've talked about ministry for our urban high schools? I have someone you need to meet." That was the first time I heard about Kevin Williams and Urban Young Life. Kevin had grown up in Cincinnati. His mom had moved him from an inner-city community to the suburbs when he was getting into trouble. At his new suburban school, Kevin was introduced to Jesus through a high school ministry called Young Life. The YL experience was so impactful that after college Kevin began volunteer leading with YL in northern Kentucky (part of Greater Cincinnati), one of the nation's most successful YL chapters.

After years there, Kevin's burden for Cincinnati's urban core schools gripped his heart. He and his wife prayerfully accepted the call to plant Greater Cincinnati Urban YL. As a biracial, bicultural young man, Kevin has terrific multicultural skills. He and Katie soon won the hearts of school administrators, teachers, parents, and students and were successful planting the first Cincy area urban YL. With a vision to multiply, they opened the second school after a few years, and that's when I learned about him. The ministry was young and small but flourishing.

That vacation phone call proved God-ordained. After meeting Kevin and hearing his story, I agreed to join a conversation of like-hearted leaders from several churches to help Kevin and Katie develop infrastructure for their fledgling, disciple-making vision. The Greater Cincinnati Urban Young Life Area Committee was born. Today the ministry includes over ten high schools across the city with multiple staff and over fifty volunteer leaders. Kevin has now moved on to a new career and has turned the ministry over to the next generation. Amazing. The church collective.

City Servants. Perhaps the most impactful local expression of collective church-like-heaven-on-earth effort in our city is a monthly round table of Kingdom servant leaders known as city servants. We began in the mid-1990s, with antecedents dating back to an urban ministries united monthly prayer group, several pastoral groups with a heart to see the whole gospel for the whole city from the whole church, and a couple of lay-led initiatives for city transformation through the gospel of Jesus Christ. This culturally, racially, denominationally, generationally, and work-life diverse group of women and men exist to connect, unite, and support any life-giving Kingdom endeavors and initiatives for deep change over decades in Cincinnati. We intentionally keep race at the center of all we do, through Christ in us, because most every societal ill needing healing and wholeness in Greater Cincinnati is exacerbated by race: historical or current racism and the racialization of life (see Mark Curnutte's *The State of Black Cincinnati 2015: Two Cities*).

This roundtable was not established by accident. There was much prayer, intentionality, mutual submission, and effort by many people over many years. What that Spirit-led work has now yielded for the work of Christ in our city is an unbelievable level of trust and transactional traction in the church collective for matters of goodness and the flourishing of our city and its population. In addition to the monthly meetings of thirty or so leaders—which are well-planned and led by a smaller microcosm of the whole—semiannually we hold a Unify Cincy lunch event of a hundred or so gospel-centered leaders. At Unify Cincy, we highlight a single theme, such as at-risk youth, mass incarceration, the heroin pandemic, or our foster care crisis. We then choose two or three best-practice practitioners to share what they're doing in the space of that day's theme and to tell us how we can pray for them. We provide time to respond in table groups of five, and we encourage networking before and after. Why? To build strength, momentum, and scale.

Culture is critical. Our culture for Kingdom work in Cincinnati is that we are *one* team. We are *for* each other. We practice the steps of Matthew 18:15-22 when we have a conflict. And we actually walk in intentional humility and unity, through Christ in us, for the sake of our King and His Kingdom, and for the sake of the wellbeing of our city. It works. And the glory is all His.

Chapter 56

NATIONAL IMPACT

In my experience, the Lord leads subtly.

I'm reminded of Elijah's experience with the Lord at Horeb (1 Kings 19). When the great and powerful wind passed by, the Lord was not in it. When the earth quaked and the rocks shattered, the Lord was not in the earthquake. Nor was He in the fire. Instead, He was in the gentle whisper.

That's my experience most of the time. It's why our early morning preparation in the Lord is so vital. At the start of every day, get low before Him. Get into worship and thanksgiving. Soak in His Word. Be filled with His Spirit. Then you are so much better postured and attentive to hear His whispers and see His hand at work. And even then, it's a matter of acting in faith, because rarely is there wind, quakes, or fire when He is leading you. Yet lead He does.

Our experience at Peoples Church Cincinnati and Network is that God is up to some pretty amazing things. And the opportunity is to say yes.

"Yes" often leads to energy, momentum, and growth in the Kingdom. "Yes" requires faith, and faith pleases the Lord (see *The Power of Yes* by Shawn Nason).

Below I have shared some testimonies of how doing church-like-heaven-on-earth has led to national engagements far beyond what our church size (about six hundred) would signal. With all my heart, I know it's because of how much the Lord is in this work.

ASSEMBLIES OF GOD NATIONAL BLACK FELLOWSHIP

I believe every Christian ministry is helped by being part of a larger network for accountability, relationship, and missional strategy. For me and Peoples Church and Network, that includes two key entities: the Assemblies of God USA, and the AG National Black Fellowship.

As a fourth generation Pentecostal and AG-connected minister (on my grandmother Beard's side), I've seen the good, the bad, and the ugly. I am reminded of Paul's wisdom: "We have this treasure in jars of clay" (2 Corinthians 4:7). This means keeping a reasonable perspective regarding the strengths and weaknesses of any network and of myself—we're all finite, sinful human beings, hopefully redeemed and being formed into the image of Christ. That said, I'm also glad I frequently hear AG leaders say, "The Kingdom of God is much bigger than the Assemblies of God." Indeed it is.

So, within the AG USA, I benefit from terrific teammates and co-leaders in Ohio, across the nation, and around the world. I also benefit from a team of African American AG ministers who organized a fellowship for the mutual edification of the whole AG.

In 2006, they allowed our church (which is 50 percent nonwhite) to join so that we could enjoy and benefit from black leadership over my life and for our congregation from within our own AG Network. In the summer of 2018, we had the very high honor of hosting the biennial conference of the AGNBF at Peoples Church in Uptown Cincinnati. AGNBF president at that time, Michael Nelson, is a dear friend, as is the new and current president, Walter Harvey. We pray together often. I love these brothers deeply; they are life-friends to me. In preparation for the 2018 REACH Conference, as the biennial meeting of the NBF is titled, Michael made a site visit in advance. On that trip, something only church collective could allow took place. Michael helped Terry Thomas, whose story I shared earlier.

Oh my.

On June 28, 2018, a cancelled flight allowed Michael to have a heart-to-heart visit with Terry, who, like Michael, grew up in the Chicago projects. They had never before met, but Michael remembered me asking prayer for Terry who needed help finding his way back to his walk with Jesus and healing from father wounds that only an older brother of color could relate to. And it happened: healing, cancelled sin, and glorious renewal as the three of us fellowshipped together over dinner sharing our lives. The extra time had only been made possible because of Michael's cancelled flight and sensitivity to the Holy Spirit to ask about meeting Terry. Neither of us knew they'd grown up in the same projects twenty years apart. God appointments. Church collective. God in the whisper.

HILLSONG SAN FRANCISCO, BRENDAN BROWN, CHURCH COLLECTIVE AND THE HOLY SPIRIT

What the Lord did in this particular story, I still can't fathom. His Holy Spirit is the real deal. The power in His church collective is real.

What happened is this: It was a Thursday text—it came immediately after we prayed concluding our SLT (senior leadership team) meeting at Peoples Uptown. But first some backdrop to this story.

A few weeks earlier that summer of 2018, Jan and I had celebrated our thirtieth wedding anniversary in San Francisco, staying downtown in the thick of the city. To our amazement and chagrin, the streets were crowded with homeless drug users and mentally ill people. We walked and watched, heartbroken, as people just aimlessly went about their day—surviving, subsisting, lost. We couldn't help but wonder, "Where is the church?"

We had learned that Hillsong SF had recently launched and met just blocks from our hotel. We walked to Sunday service there, as we often do when in a Hillsong city. The familiar, warm, life-giving flow of the Kingdom was present, as usual. We love Hillsong.

How encouraged I was when the pastor welcomed the crowd and said, "It looks like heaven in here! I love the array of cultures and ethnicities gathered in this room under Jesus." My heart leapt. For years I've been praying about a greater connection to Hillsong for church-like-heaven-on-earth, in the whole earth. They multiply their work so well and bring such sound theological content in their worship. But never had I heard such an intentional articulation from Revelation 7:9. Most churches see it as a nice bonus if it happens; they don't realize the power of intent and content of God's actual strategy through His diversely united purchase.

It just so happens that on this same Sunday, back home, Peoples Church was on the front page of the *Cincinnati Enquirer*, highlighted by a picture of an older white man (my predecessor, Clyde Miller) and a younger man of color embracing, connecting, being the church. The story was underscoring the work of the racially reconciling gospel in several Cincinnati churches, as well as the small group curriculum toward that end, *Undivided*, out of Crossroads Church and developed by my dear friend Chuck Mingo and his team. (Later that summer, the story would run in *USA Today*, depicting Chuck Mingo on the front page.)

After the Hillsong SF service, I was standing on the entry steps outside waiting for Jan who stood in line for the facilities (yes, a nine-month-old church already bursting at the seams). I was prayerfully observing Pastor Brenden love on people, pouring out enormous amounts of energy between services. He caught my eye and stopped over to greet this apparent new-comer/observer. Before ninety seconds passed, we had exchanged contact info. I simply affirmed him for what his leadership had meant to me that morning already, and then, following a whisper I heard in my heart, I mentioned Crossroads, *Undivided*, and Peoples Church; the attention that the Revelation 7:9 and John 17:21 church garners in the eyes of the world; and what if in the year 2033 (the 2000-year ascension anniversary, at least according to the Gregorian calendar) there was a global live worship service? The global body would likely want Hillsong to be a key convener.

I know, that's a lot to say just upon first meeting someone. But that's what poured out.

Later that month, I got a text from Brenden. It wasn't about a global worship meeting or anything like that. It was just this: "Chris, just want you to know you're on my heart right now for prayer."

God whispers.

In that very SLT meeting, I had needed to share some very heavy news related to a staff and church family situation (the one that just a week or so later blew up as N. T. Wright and I exchanged emails about this biblical prescription and vision of church). We had just cried out to the Lord for His help and for wisdom, and in that very moment of saying the "amen," Brenden texted.

God whispers.

The next day Brenden explained to me the timing of his message. He was returning from Australia and, as the plane was landing, he felt the Holy Spirit nudge him to pray for me. That coming weekend, he would be preaching on how the Spirit speaks to us and would be encouraging Hillsong SF to act on the small impressions, the whispers. We rejoiced together as we talked—at how amazing our God is! Before we ended the call, I asked if I could share with him our burden for the crises of homelessness, addiction, and mental health that we had seen in San Francisco just a few weeks earlier. The question that pulsated in my heart: Where is the church? I told him it was after that cry out to the Lord that we found out that Hillsong SF was meeting there on Nob Hill just blocks away from our hotel. Immediately Brenden exclaimed, "We're a young church, but you're right, we have to get involved." The good news is, when the church works collectively as one in a city, together we are mature and massive, full of manifold wisdom (Ephesians 3:9-10). Today we pray for the leadership of young churches planting in major cities, that God will give them the wisdom and the humility to servant lead broader movements for the greater good in their cities (Jeremiah 29:7).

God whispers.

OHIO FOR JESUS, THE OHIO MINISTRY NETWORK AG

We were preparing our executive presbyter retreat for late 2014. I was serving as the southwest Ohio regional presbyter/overseer for my missional and accountability network, the Assemblies of God. I was one of seven on the EP team. The General Superintendent of Tanzania, Barnabas Mtokambali, was visiting Peoples Church in Cincinnati. Earlier that year, we had served together for his top leaders' meeting in Tanzania. He had invited me to teach on theology of missions, but what I saw and learned was an incredible, prayerful, and strategic planning process for multiplying leaders and churches across a nation. Tanzania for Jesus, they called their ten-year strategic plan—10,000 new leaders, 10,000 new churches by 2020. Wow. And they were on schedule.

So now Barnabas, aptly named, was available to join us at our EP retreat. It was just a gentle whisper on my heart from the Lord. Our Ohio leader and superintendent, John Wootton, a humble godly leader himself, welcomed the man to our retreat. At the end of our first evening session, John invited Pastor Barnabas to pray for us. When he did, he slid out of his chair to his knees. Before he was done praying, we were all kneeling. With his Nelson Mandela voice and demeanor, Barnabas called out to heaven for us, for the lost in our state, and for the transformation of Ohio in the name of Jesus.

Our hearts were fastened together. A continental African leader and seven Midwest pastors from the American heartland. Little did we know how significant to our work this prayer meeting would turn out to be. Suffice it to say, a partnership was birthed that holds significant Kingdom ramifications for Ohio for the decade to come.

This story is really John Wootton's to tell, so let me here just say this: John ended up leading forty-four pastors and presbyters on a momentous multi-day retreat to Tanzania. We saw what the Tanzania AG team is accomplishing there, and we met for our own strategic planning under their leadership, along with one of our own USAG strategic planning experts assisting with cultural translation. In the end, we adopted a very similar larger-than-life, data-based, prayer-birthed ten-year strategic plan of our own to multiply leaders and churches and see the cities and counties of Ohio experiencing healing, wholeness, and life through the power of the gospel of Jesus Christ.

We are launching this statewide initiative with goals unlike we've ever dreamed before, toward a 2030 completion. We are doing so with an increasingly diverse OMN leadership team, a better reflection of all of Ohio and the Kingdom, and all of this catalyzed by the Lord through a man of color whose home is thousands of miles away and in a culture far different from our own. Church-like-heaven-on-earth. Manifold wisdom. And each key piece of Ohio for Jesus has started with leaders responding to a gentle whisper of God.

COMPASSION COUNCIL AND AG BLACK LEADERSHIP

In 2007, the Assemblies of God elected our first pastor of color to the national leadership team of six, the ELT (Executive Leadership Team). Zollie Smith became the national director of what we call US Missions. In his acceptance speech at that national conference, Zollie trumpeted a clarion call to the "highways and the byways" of American, that no one would ever be left out of God's plan of salvation. His ten-year theme for AG US Missions became "That None Perish."

My heart was so filled with joy.

Zollie and I had become friends some years before when he was the only pastor in the AG network who could give me a reference regarding Pastor Ezra Maize, the first pastor of color to join our staff at Peoples Church back in 2001. At the time, Pastor Zollie was serving in New Jersey leadership, and it was there he'd come to know Ezra. I felt so much respect for him right from that first call. He encouraged me. He encouraged the vision in me as I articulated it the best I could considering how early we were in the process of it all, with so few models to look to, and while our church was still 98 percent white. But Zollie respected that we were going somewhere meaningful and said, "Chris, do it!"

Later in 2006, while serving as president, he wholeheartedly welcomed me and our church into the AG National Black Fellowship when we were still only 15 percent people of color. I love this man so much.

Now he was one of our six national leaders, and the Assemblies of God would not look back with regard to biblical diverse inclusion at the top (as of this writing there are now two ethnic minorities and a woman serving in the ELT; still needing a Jewish descent representative, as far as I know). This is important, not only because of the theology of church-like-heaven-on-earth and the apologetic it is for the gospel of Jesus Christ, but also because our three million US constituency alone is now 42 percent ethnic minority, and over half women, not to mention the sixty-six million AG adherents in the rest of the non-Caucasian majority world.

And now as our US Missions director, Zollie set his heart to include the "least of those among us." He set out to establish a national board, a compassion council, of diverse practitioners serving orphans (foster kids), the elderly, the physically disabled, the mentally ill, the refugees, the immigrants, the urban poor, the rural poor, the trafficked. We met twice annually for three years in the mid-2010s. My contribution was for foster care. For years, we had been seeing a movement grow in Cincinnati of believers wrapping their hearts and lives around vulnerable kids, and churches supporting those fearless, selfless families. Zollie's compassion council met to encourage each other, network, strategize, and scale our work across the nation through the local church. Indeed, Kingdom work pleasing a generous, compassionate, and just almighty King, blessing society, and making the name of Jesus more famous.

I think back to the first phone call to Pastor Zollie in New Jersey. It was like a God whisper of so much more to come. The latent power for the Kingdom of racially reconciling church.

CHI ALPHA, DIVERSITY COUNCIL

University ministries have a prime opportunity to make disciples of all peoples. Not only because of the ethnic, national, and language diversity on American campuses, but because young people are so open to the inclusion of others. When the gospel itself is shown to be for everyone by the very nature of the group makeup, students are drawn. What a proof of John 17:21—"Father unite them so the world will believe" (my paraphrase), a national implication for church-like-heaven-on-earth.

Belkis and Steve Lehman, who serve with Chi Alpha College ministries of the AG, have taken up this vision. It began simply enough. Our University of Cincinnati Chi Alpha leader at the time, Sadell Bradley, an African American woman, asked where all the black leaders were. She had recently attended a regional conference led by the Lehmans, and she was the only person of color. The next year, Belkis and Sadell held a one-day African American Leadership Conference, inviting students from across the Great Lakes Region. We didn't know if there would be ten students or zero. There were seventy!

Before long, Belkis was named the national diversity specialist for Chi Alpha. Sadell moved on to plant a church with her husband, Sherman, while Belkis formed a national diversity council. Brandon Wilkes, who with his wife, Dorothy, leads Peoples Church St. Louis and serves on our Peoples Network eldership, stepped into the slot vacated by Sadell to assist Belkis in building this vision.

Here's the significance: hundreds and thousands of women and men of color and immigrant or international backgrounds are coming to Christ in and through Chi Alpha across the nation. As they are becoming leaders, filled with the Holy Spirit and on fire for the King and His Kingdom, they are feeling called into local church leadership, campus ministry leadership, marketplace leadership, and international missions leadership. The US-based gospel ministry force is about to be populated more diversely than ever in the history of the Assemblies of God network.

Further, Belkis and Steve decided to leave their role as regional Chi Alpha directors and pioneer new campuses again. They've dived in with HBCUs (Historic Black Colleges and Universities) in North Carolina. The harvest is ripe. Like Jesus with the woman at the well in Samaria (a woman from a mixed-race people not considered worthy of ministry by the Jewish disciples), Jesus saw fields full unto harvest (John 4).

As ethnic minority young people are entering the vocational, especially support-raising, ministry fields, many new hindrances and barriers have revealed themselves—challenges to be wisely overcome. Already the Lehmans and the Diversity Council have developed the Minority Mobilization Fund—a genius solution to an inherent reality, especially for African Americans who come from 10 percent of the net worth of white Americans on average (see Michael O. Emerson's books, articles, and studies). Additionally, their churches have naturally had to focus at home in light of the American black experience of oppression and resultant income and asset disadvantages. Please find in the Resource List at the end lists of articles and books on the subject for wisdom in overcoming these said challenges.

Sadell had just asked a question. Belkis, who is of Cuban descent herself, responded proactively. God whispers, people act in faith, and profound change and Kingdom increase is produced.

Chapter 57

GLOBAL IMPACT

Like the church in Antioch, diversely reconciled teams of Jesus worshipers can make monumental ripples into the earth. The leadership team alone was noteworthy for its unlikely makeup: Lucius of Cyrene (North Africa), Simeon called Niger (literally, "black man"), Paul and Barnabas (Jews, and from very different tribes, Benjamin and Levi, and places—Tarsus and Cyprus), and finally, Manaen—a Gentile, raised in wealth as part of Herod's household (Acts 13:1-5). It was this richly united team that sent out the missionary endeavor that forever changed history.

In similar ways, when the Spirit is speaking as the Lord is being worshiped by a kaleidoscope of people, movement takes place—outward movement of the rule of Jesus. Consider the Azusa Street Revival from 1906–1908 and how many thousands of lives were set ablaze to carry the gospel to the ends of the earth. A small meeting space, but an enormous impact out of women and men, white, black, brown, and from different language backgrounds worshiping as one, with heaven coming down to meet them and send them. And send them He did. Any cursory study of those days reveals the missionary stirring and the heart of God for the nations that was engendered in the diverse worship there and acted upon.

So today, a more fully orbed theology of missions is gaining traction: *the whole church taking the whole gospel into the whole world together.* On its face, it's just a matter of practical wisdom: All the talent of the church involved and her collective wisdom applied for finishing the Kingdom tasks (Matthew 24:14). Further, it's spiritually and apologetically strategic, albeit not easy. Jesus prayed that the Father would make us one so that the world will believe (see John 17:21). How will the world see our *oneness* in Christ if we're not *one* on a practical level of personal friendships—fellowshipping, learning, and living the Kingdom together in diverse unity? The hidden power of the reconciling gospel, which reconciles people to the Father and to one another, is that unlikely friends who once were enemies (or at least very differentiated and separate from one another) are now united. That's a compelling testimony—quite an evidence that Jesus really is the Messiah (John 17:21-23). It's not easy. In fact, it's messy and hard, but it also drives back the darkness unlike any other strategy (Ephesians 3:9-10). Driven-back darkness can't hold people captive to itself any longer. See why this is so powerful?

Already we see the beginning of change in the US missionary thinking and strategy. I see it in AG World missions for one. And I'm certain this emerging change is not exclusive to the Assemblies of God. It's just not like God only to work in one gospel-centered group apart from others who are all part of the same team anyway—Jesus' team.

Examples of Intentional Ethnic/Economic Diversification and Inclusion

USAGWM diversity and inclusion efforts

» Diverse working groups are studying questions around how to accomplish recruitment and on ramping up of ethnic minority global missionaries from the US AG. The US AG constituency is 42 percent ethnic minorities, yet our world missionary force is less than 2 percent (2018).

» Specific regions of USAGWM are inviting leaders of ethnic and language minority fellowships to consider how their on-field team and leadership cultures will need to change for inclusion of minorities as equals.

» Further, there is much thought being given to the financial and support-raising realities of historically oppressed minority groups. What special and intentional solutions, culturally and systemically, must be considered to ensure the success of diverse inclusion and unity?

AG World Fellowship

» Could intentionally diverse missions teams, serving together strategically across the earth among unreached people groups (Joshua Project definition), push back the spiritual darkness, make disciples, and teach and preach the gospel of the Kingdom (Matthew 24:14)? According to Ephesians 3:4-6, 9-10, yes!

» The AG World Fellowship in 2018 represented 69 million believers in Jesus. Yet, by far the majority of these are not involved in global missions. The latent missionary force, talent pool, and resource potential in very sense of that word *resource* is like a sleeping giant with respect to missionary impact against the task of reaching the remaining 42 percent unreached, 7000 UPGs (JoshuaProject.net).

» With respect to the remaining task of Bible translation alone, this largely unengaged, diverse team could dramatically come alongside. What if?

In effect, I'm asking the question, and using the Assemblies of God as one example. Imagine if the whole church was ministering the whole gospel together in diversely united teams in the whole earth among every people. It might just lead to fulfillment of the Great Commission. Which leads us to the next chapter.

PART VI

Endgame—Back to Theology

We can approach this biblical topic of diversely united church in many different ways: the story of Peoples Church Cincinnati; the theology; the societal need; the need of the universal church to become who she is called to be and to accomplish what she's been purchased for by His blood; the description of how the earth would be different and will be different. All of these are different angles from which we could come to the content of this book.

Allow me for a moment to go back to the story in Acts 20 that we discussed in chapter 1. Remember that Paul had called for a meeting of the elders of Ephesus. He was on his last trip back to Jerusalem. But on the way there, he had the ship pull into the Miletus harbor. From that coastal town, he called for a meeting of the Ephesian elders. They come from twenty miles or so north. You may want to take a minute to reread the story.

Paul poured out his heart to the elders. He reminded them of all that he had taught them—the whole will or counsel of God. He warned them with all intensity: Defend what you've been given! People will try to tear this up. Don't let it happen!

What drove Paul to stop and make sure he had this final meeting with the Ephesian leaders whom he had lived among and taught so earnestly for three years? What was this "whole will of God" that Paul referred to in Acts 20:27? Remember, Paul's letter to the Ephesians lays out what he could have been referring to in the Acts account, as I unpacked in chapter 2 of this book—the Lord's strategic plan in the earth. Paul even posits that this "one new humanity" is the "mystery of Christ, which . . . has now been revealed" (Ephesians 2:15; 3:4-6). There *is* mystery to it.

Which brings me to another window through which to view this vision of church—one that is a lot more prophetic or metaphorical and less didactic, if you will, but no less scriptural. We view this prophetic scene through a study of *two temples*: John's in Revelation and Ezekiel's. Starting with the one in Ezekiel, I'd like to dive into this metaphorical/prophetic expression for the dwelling of our Lord here as we're coming to a close.

You may want to have your Bible out for this next section to look at the Scriptures for yourself as we move along.

If you're like me, you've always wondered about the temple described in Ezekiel 40–47. After all, it is a temple that has never been built. Why has God provided such extraordinary detail for Ezekiel to describe this never-built temple? Many have made some attempts at fitting it into certain eschatological frameworks, but at a very basic level, it's just a mystery.

Ezekiel's temple has never been built—it's not Solomon's temple, or Ezra's, or Herod's—but does it prefigure a temple in the New City, the Revelation 21 New Jerusalem? This solution has one problem—Revelation 21:22 says the city has no temple because the Lord God Almighty and the Lamb are its temple!

So, what is this temple in Ezekiel? Could it be a *prefiguring* of the temple of the Lord in the New Covenant, the people of God themselves?

Ephesians 2:21 says, "In him the whole *building* is joined together and rises to become a *holy temple* in the Lord" (emphasis mine).

What building? The *one new humanity* created in Himself, Jews and nations, members *together* of His household, built on the foundation of the apostles and prophets, with Christ Jesus Himself the chief cornerstone (see Ephesians 2:14-22).

Now, one more critical piece.

Once while studying Ezekiel 43 and seeking the Lord in preparation for writing this book, I couldn't leave Ezekiel 43:8-11 for several days. I was again and again prayerfully meditating over these verses: "Son of man, describe the temple to the people of Israel, that they may be ashamed of their sins. Let them consider its perfection, and if they are ashamed of all they have done, make known to them the design of the temple—its arrangement, its exits and entrances—its whole design and all its regulations and laws"—when all of a sudden this realization hit me: Ezekiel was not talking about a physical temple in physical Jerusalem. He was prophesying about God's people as the *temple of the Lord*. I immediately felt prompted (a gentle whisper) to look at Ephesians 2:21, "In him the whole building is joined together and rises to become a holy temple in the Lord." Paul had even said, "Members of his household, built on the foundation of the apostles and the *prophets*" (Ephesians 2:19-20, emphasis mine).

Now, I don't know if by "prophets" Paul meant early church prophets (see 1 Corinthians 12:28) or the Old Testament prophets, or both! But we know that the Lord often taught from the Scriptures about the Kingdom and about Himself, and the only Scriptures either He or Paul had available to that point was the Old Testament (Luke 24:27).

At that insight moment, the way it looked to me was this: Both Ezekiel and Paul were speaking spiritual words about the same holy temple of the Lord.

I was stunned. Still am.

From my view, two major inspirations were converging: Paul's meeting with the Ephesian elders on the beach at Miletus (the "whole plan/will of God" discourse, Acts 20:27; the diversely united one new humanity *soma* [body] of nations and Jews in Ephesians 2:15, *the mystery of Christ* now revealed in Ephesians 3:4-6) *and* Ezekiel's 43:10-11 temple description.

The Lord was telling Ezekiel, "Make known to [my people] the design of the temple," make known its perfection (Ezekiel 43:10-11), and Paul was saying to the Ephesian elders, "I have not hesitated to proclaim to you the whole will of God," with tears and trembling, night and day over three years (Acts 20:17–21:1).

And as I just highlighted a moment ago from his letter to the same Ephesians where I believe Paul outlines that very plan/will of God in detail, Paul called them "a holy temple" (Ephesians 2:21).

So in a very real sense we've actually discussed three temples: Ezekiel's temple, the temple of Revelation 21, and the temple of believers in Paul's theology (Ephesians 2:21).

And—stay with me on this—it's the New Jerusalem's *lack of* a temple (Revelation 21) that brings it all together (the three temples) or more accurately said, the fact that "the Lord God Almighty and the Lamb are its temple" (Revelation 21:22). Whose temple? The Holy City's temple, the New Jerusalem's temple—the city John saw *as a bride* dressed for her husband (Revelation 21:2). What is the temple in the Holy City, the New Jerusalem, the Bride? The Lamb and the Lord God Almighty.

Selah.

So the temple in the end of the age is the Lamb and the Lord God Almighty, and rivers of living water flow from the throne of God and of the Lamb (Revelation 21:22; 22:1).

So each of these temple passages from Ezekiel to Ephesians to Revelation provides crucial insight with respect to God's strategic plan. *Each of these temples has rivers of living water* flowing out from within them (Ezekiel 47; John 7:38; Revelation 22). In Ezekiel and Revelation, the rivers nourish trees bearing fruit and leaves for healing (Ezekiel 47:12; Revelation 22:2).

While not as explicit as to be called a river of life by Paul, this idea of fecundity from the indwelling Spirit in the life of the believers, individually and collectively, does resonate in Pauline theology.

How? By what the Spirit produces in and through us—that same Spirit who fills the diversely united church as well as individual believers (Ephesians 5:18) and who nourishes spiritual fruit (Galatians 5:22-25) and spiritual gifts (1 Corinthians 12) in and through us, both personally and as the diversely united one new humanity. We are one reconciled body, His household, a whole building, a holy temple, a dwelling in which God lives by His Spirit (Ephesians 2).

For Ezekiel, the river teeming with life flows from under the threshold of the temple (Ezekiel 47:1), which is also the place of God's throne (Ezekiel 43:7), the seat of His rulership.

For Paul and for John in his Gospel, the living waters and resultant fruit and gifts (or the Spirit flow) is from wellsprings within the believers (John 7:38; 1 Corinthian 12; Galatians 5:22-25; Ephesians 5:18), who like Ezekiel's temple also have God's rulership over their lives.

For John in Revelation, the river of the water of life flows from under the throne of the Lord God Almighty and the Lamb, who are its temple at the center of the Holy City, which is His bride (Revelation 21:2, 9, 22).

For all three, there are rivers of living water that team with life flowing out. For all three, there is the power and presence of God's rulership.

Remember that Jesus said, "In your own Law it is written that the testimony of two witnesses is true" (John 8:17).

So don't just take my word for any of this. Study these passages and these threads for yourself and see what the Lord speaks to your own heart. I'm simply sharing what I saw and heard in my own spirit as I wrestled with Ezekiel 43.

If you're like me, you need some time to think on this and look at these passages. As you do, invite the Holy Spirit to illuminate what you are reading. If what I think I'm seeing about all of this is wrong, please let me know, and thanks for reading this book!

So what have we been talking about?

I believe Scripture reveals a comprehensive plan and purpose of God for His church—how it's designed, what it's to be, and what all it should do and accomplish. I believe it is a comprehensive "design" with many specifics.

For Ezekiel, it was to "describe the temple to the people of Israel, that they may be ashamed of their sins. Let them consider its perfection" (Ezekiel 43:10).

For Paul, it was his letter to the Ephesians, the mystery of Christ revealed (Ephesians 3:4-6).

For John, it all comes together in Revelation 21 and 22, a new city, a bride.

Paul refers to it as one new humanity, a body, a household, a building, a temple. John sees a Holy City, a New Jerusalem, a bride.

I believe we've inadvertently missed the richness and specificity of it all. I know I did.

Here's my most important point: I believe the Scriptures show us the Lord's strategy of temple, of bride, of one new humanity, of the mystery of Christ now revealed, as an *endgame*. Let's drive back to the profound statement Paul makes to the Ephesian elders in Acts 20:27, "I have not hesitated to proclaim to *you* the whole will of God" (emphasis mine).

I believe the *endgame* is alluded to in Ephesians 1:18-23:

> I pray that the eyes of your heart may be enlightened in order that you may know the hope to which he has called you, the riches of his glorious inheritance in his holy people, and his incomparably great power for us who believe. That power is the same as the mighty strength he exerted when he raised Christ from the dead and seated him at his right hand in the heavenly realms, far above all rule and authority, power and dominion, and every name that is invoked, not only in the present age but also in the one to come. *And God placed all things under his feet and appointed him to be head over everything for the church, which is his body*, the fullness of him who fills everything in every way. (emphasis mine)

The endgame.

To me, it means that from the time of the resurrection forward, and from the time of the Spirit's outpouring until the end of the age, every enemy of Christ, and all things, are being brought under His authority, His rulership.

He extends His rulership on earth through gospel-transformed lives and fully gospel-centered and Spirit-filled believers and churches. This is especially true when the church is functioning not only according to His character but also profoundly functioning in congruence with His strategic design/plan.

For more evidence, let's look to Hebrews 2:8: "'YOU HAVE PUT ALL THINGS IN SUBJECTION UNDER HIS FEET.' For in subjecting all things to him, He left nothing that is not subject to him. *But now we do not yet see all things subjected to him*" (NASB, emphasis mine).

So, based on Hebrews 2, the work is both done and not *yet* done. The process is not complete. All things are being subjected to Him, but are not yet so. This is George Eldon Ladd's, "Already, but not yet." The Kingdom is here, but it's not yet fully realized and is progressing until the end of the age. (See *A Theology of the New Testament*, by G. E. Ladd.)

First Corinthians 15 also provides helpful insight:

> Then comes the end, when He hands over the kingdom to the God and Father, when He has abolished all rule and all authority and power. For He must reign until He has put all His enemies under His feet. The last enemy that will be abolished is death. FOR HE HAS PUT ALL THINGS IN SUBJECTION UNDER HIS FEET. But when He says, "All things are put in subjection," it is evident that He is excepted who put all things in subjection to Him. When all things are subjected to Him, then the Son Himself also will be subjected to the One who subjected all things to Him, so that God may be all in all. (1 Corinthians 15:24-28, NASB)

Everything is being placed under Jesus' authority to be given over to the Father. How? *Through His church* (Ephesians 1:22)—not through politics or taking over earthly governments because Jesus said, "My kingdom is not of this world" (John 18:36). Instead, His Kingdom will come through the expansion of the Kingdom of God through the full gospel of Jesus Christ in the hearts of individual lives, in families, and through His church in communities, in cities, and in nations. What kind of church? His diversely united church exercising the fullness of His gospel in every way, personally and in every facet of society. That's the quality of church that has the authority, the fullness, the "whole will of God."

Through *this* church, the rulers, authorities, powers of this dark world, and spiritual forces of evil in the spiritual realm (Ephesians 6:12) take notice (Ephesians 3:10). The enemies of Christ are brought into subjection under the rule of Jesus. The Kingdom of God advances toward a 1 Corinthians 15:25 completion in the earth and heavens. The Corinthian church receiving the letter of 1 Corinthians was itself a beautiful collection of diverse others united through the gospel. It was to *them* that Paul explained the *endgame* in 1 Corinthians 15:24-28, the same *endgame* alluded to in Ephesians 1:22!

That letter, 1 Corinthians, was written by Paul *from Ephesus* where he had spent three years teaching night and day, with tears, the "whole will" (complete plan) of God.

See the significance of that Ephesian church model, and why Paul is so adamant in Acts 20 about what they have?

Another insight around this idea that spiritual strongholds are being destroyed by the Lord through diversely inclusive, gospel-centered groups of believers might be gained from the story of the mob riot in Thessalonica described in Acts 17:6: "These men . . . have caused trouble all over the world." Who said that and why?

It was said by the Jewish leaders who were jealous that Paul's teaching was turning societal and religious norms on their head. Just look at the text:

> When Paul and his companions had passed through Amphipolis and Apollonia, they came to Thessalonica, where there was a Jewish synagogue. As was his custom, Paul went into the synagogue, and on three Sabbath days he reasoned with them from the Scriptures, explaining and proving that the Messiah had to suffer and rise from the dead. "This Jesus I am proclaiming to you is the Messiah," he said. *Some of the Jews were persuaded and joined Paul and Silas, as did a large number of God-fearing Greeks and quite a few prominent women.*
>
> But other Jews were jealous; so they rounded up some bad characters from the marketplace, formed a mob and started a riot in the city. They rushed to Jason's house in search of Paul and Silas in order to bring them out to the crowd. But when they did not find them, they dragged Jason and some other believers before the city officials, shouting: "These men who have caused trouble all over the world [have turned the world upside down, KJV] have now come here." (Acts 17:1-6, emphasis mine)

Luke (the author of Acts) was reporting that Paul's vision and calling to preach a gospel that includes nations along with Jews, women equal with men, the people of God together in Jesus of Nazareth, the Messiah, caused rioting because the world's ways were being rocked wherever these men preached.

Even Paul's eventual arrest in Jerusalem was on these same grounds. Look at *that* story again:

> When the seven days were nearly over, some Jews from the province of Asia saw Paul at the temple. They stirred up the whole crowd and

seized him, shouting, "Fellow Israelites, help us! This is the man who teaches everyone everywhere against our people and our law and this place. And besides, he has brought Greeks into the temple and defiled this holy place." (*They had previously seen Trophimus the Ephesian in the city with Paul and assumed that Paul had brought him into the temple.*)

The whole city was aroused, and the people came running from all directions. Seizing Paul, they dragged him from the temple, and immediately the gates were shut. While they were trying to kill him, news reached the commander of the Roman troops that the whole city of Jerusalem was in an uproar. He at once took some officers and soldiers and ran down to the crowd. When the rioters saw the commander and his soldiers, they stopped beating Paul.

The commander came up and arrested him and ordered him to be bound with two chains. Then he asked who he was and what he had done. (Acts 21:27–33, emphasis mine)

Trophimus was a Gentile from Ephesus. The Jewish leaders stirred up a crowd against Paul because they believed he had practiced Gentile inclusion at the temple itself. They didn't arrest him for preaching Jesus as the Messiah, which of course he did, but because he was known for a gospel that included Gentiles as recipients of the promises to Israel!

The authorities, rulers, and powers of this dark world and the spiritual forces of evil in the heavenly realms hate this message!

You see, the strategy of God is diverse unity in one body of nations and Jews through the power of the Cross and the Resurrection that turns the world upside down.

That's still true. And it's the strategy to the end of the age.

One final exclamation point. In Revelation 10, the angel with the last trumpet is standing with one foot on the land and the other on the sea. He holds a small scroll. He's about to blow the final trumpet. The endgame is near.

But first, with right hand raised to heaven, he swears by the One who lives forever and ever, who created the heavens and all that is in them. Then he says, "There will be no more delay!" (Revelation 10:6b)

No more delay for what?

"But in the days when the seventh angel is about to sound his trumpet [the last trumpet], the *mystery of God will be accomplished*, just as he announced to his servants the prophets" (Revelation 10:7, emphasis mine).

The mystery of God? We know what that is from Ephesians 3:4-6, which we discussed earlier in chapter 2.

John is saying that it will be accomplished, the mystery of God, and without any further delay.

Remember, at the writing of Revelation, John had just been exiled to Patmos from Ephesus, about forty-five miles out to sea from the famous port city. The ethos, theology, ecclesiology, and power of the Ephesian model, where Paul taught the whole will of God, must have been resonating within John's being. He pastored that same church for twenty years, following Timothy and Paul.

Now, in Revelation 10, as the Spirit leads him, John is prompted by a voice in heaven to take the little scroll from the angel's hand. This is a different scroll than the one in Revelation 5 opened by the Lamb that was slain. The contents of this scroll are not yet known to John.

So John asks for the little scroll. The angel tells him to eat it. When John eats it, what tastes good in his mouth also hurts him in his inner being (Revelation 10:10), as if to indicate this message is exciting but comes at a cost.

Then John hears, "You must prophesy *again* about many peoples, nations, languages and kings" (Revelation 10:11, emphasis mine).

The word *again* here, describes the idea of struggle or wrestling (Greek, *palae*) until which time the opponent is pinned down with hand upon his neck (Strongs NT G3823).

Now, please read the next chapter, Revelation 11, in view of what I was just emphasizing from Revelation 10.

The use of "two witnesses" in Revelation 11 alludes to the law of God that "a matter must be established by the testimony of two or three witnesses" (Deuteronomy 19:15).

In Revelation 11:1-5, the two witnesses are two olive trees (fuel supply) and two lampstands (light) standing before the Lord of the earth. Fire comes from their mouths and devours their enemies.

In Revelation 11:15, the seventh angel sounds his trumpet (the endgame is now here) and loud voices in heaven are heard saying, "The kingdom of the world has become the kingdom of our Lord and of his Messiah, and he will reign forever and ever." Praise the Lord!

Consider that thousands of years before the above actions are anywhere near complete, David prophesied in Psalm 110:

> The LORD says to my lord: "Sit at my right hand until I make your enemies a footstool for your feet." The LORD will extend your mighty scepter from Zion, saying, "Rule in the midst of your enemies!" Your troops will be willing on your day of battle. Arrayed in holy splendor, your young men will come to you like dew from the morning's womb. The LORD has sworn and will not change his mind: "You are a priest forever, in the order of Melchizedek." The Lord is at your right hand; he will crush kings on the day of his wrath. He will judge the nations, heaping up the dead and crushing the rulers of the whole earth. He will drink from a brook along the way, and so he will lift his head high.

The strategic plan of God fully unfolded. Game over.

Selah.

This is a lot to process.

Please take your time, and prayerfully consider all of these many passages in light of the thesis of this whole book, predicated on Acts 20, Ephesians 2 and 3, and Revelation 5:9-10.

And finally this: Jesus has paid with His blood for a people of every tribe, tongue, and nation to make them a priesthood and a Kingdom and is reigning now putting all His enemies under His feet, the last one to be destroyed being death, then to hand everything over to the Father, so that God may be all in all (1 Corinthians 15:28).

And we know from Revelation 21–22, there will be flourishing beyond any imagination in the new heaven and new earth. He is making everything new. Those who are victorious will inherit all this, and He will be our God and we will be His children (Revelation 21:5-7).

The kingdoms of this world are becoming the Kingdom of our Lord and of His Messiah, and He will reign forever and ever (Revelation 11:15).

"You must prophesy again about many peoples, nations, languages and kings" (Revelation 10:11).

PART VII

Challenges and Hindrances

FEAR

Fear is a huge barrier to overcome when leading any kind of change. What if it doesn't work? What if it doesn't go well? What if I don't know how to lead a church/ministry or plant a church/ministry in successful diverse unity?

Because of fear, you must have this call to lead change rooted in theology, ecclesiology, and missiology—not to mention the voice of the Lord in your inner being. Any other motivation will not sustain you when the going gets tough. You will also experience exhilarating confirmations all along the way that the Lord is in this, that this really is what His gospel requires and provides.

COSTS

As in every ministry initiative, along the way will be tangible costs—to your person, finances, friendships, and sense of identity. Look at the prices Paul paid. He actually listed them:

> Are they servants of Christ? (I am out of my mind to talk like this.) I am more. I have worked much harder, been in prison more frequently, been flogged more severely, and been exposed to death again and again. Five times I received from the Jews the forty lashes minus one. Three times I was beaten with rods, once I was pelted with stones, three times

I was shipwrecked, I spent a night and a day in the open sea, I have been constantly on the move. I have been in danger from rivers, in danger from bandits, in danger from my fellow Jews, in danger from Gentiles; in danger in the city, in danger in the country, in danger at sea; and in danger from false believers. I have labored and toiled and have often gone without sleep; I have known hunger and thirst and have often gone without food; I have been cold and naked. Besides everything else, I face daily the pressure of my concern for all the churches. Who is weak, and I do not feel weak? Who is led into sin, and I do not inwardly burn? If I must boast, I will boast of the things that show my weakness. (2 Corinthians 11:23-30)

Remember from the end game chapter (Acts 20), Paul's sufferings were usually related to the fact his gospel radically altered societal norms, bringing enemies of Christ under His feet. So backlash will come from our own flesh and blood as well as from our own humanity that struggles against the idea of a gospel that calls us to lay down our lives, our rights, our preferences to unite through Jesus with others who are not like us at all. The costs are real, and they must be counted. But those expenses are far outweighed by the blessings experienced now and in the age to come, from joining Him in establishing church-like-heaven-on-earth and all its Kingdom implications.

ECHO CHAMBERS

These are a *huge* hindrance to be overcome. When the gospel of reconciliation—understanding personal and societal righteousness—is proclaimed, people can struggle to understand the plight of others in the body whose experiences are different from their own, because they don't yet live in any expression of diverse unity. We tend to live in echo chambers that reinforce our worldviews rather than allowing our worldviews to be profoundly transformed by the Word of God. To overcoming this hindrance, we need to help free people from their echo chambers so they can listen to those different from themselves. This will help bring the whole church together diversely, with our many-faceted perspectives, and also help the church better understand, love, and evangelize outsiders. Beware of distractions.

Jesus' parable of the sower refers to the seeds that fall among the thorns and grow up but then are choked out by the cares, pleasures, and pressures of this world. Many people, activities, and concerns will attempt to distract and dissuade you from this vision. Let your prayer life and your Word life keep you centered and focused for your part in this work.

WARFARE BROADSIDES

Earlier I shared some of the spiritual warfare blows that we've experienced. I could easily write dozens more. Suffice it to say that a normal and expected part of this strategic Kingdom-building work is that you will experience blows from our enemy and his team. Set your heart on the things of God. Keep your own life protected via the wisdom of the spiritual armor laid out in Ephesians 6 and follow good practices of staying healthy, humble, and hopeful in Christ. James reminds us this way: "Consider it pure joy, my brothers and sisters, whenever you face trials of many kinds, because you know that the testing of your faith produces perseverance. Let perseverance finish its work so that you may be mature and complete, not lacking anything" (James 1:2-4). I don't think I can overemphasize the power of this passage in my own life and ministry.

IGNORANCE

Ignorance of Scripture, history, culture, economics, and ethnicities all contribute their own challenges. So, being a Christian who reads and studies the Word deeply but also reads diversely with respect to missions, history, and societal challenges from diverse perspectives is critical. When Paul ministered in Athens, he was able to connect because he studied Athenian ways of thinking about philosophy and religion. He had a sense of how to connect their perspectives with the gospel of Jesus Christ. As people of the Kingdom, that example is fantastic for us to follow.

APATHY

We can easily be so comfortable and at peace with our own salvation and the health of our church, ministry, or city that we ignore the Great Commission and the pressing matters of the Kingdom of God. This hindrance of apathy has to be acknowledged, confronted, and thwarted.

DISTRUST (LOVE ALWAYS TRUSTS)

Finally, though this is not an exhaustive list, we have seen distrust undermine the momentum and/or unity of the gospel effort. To apply 1 Corinthians 13 with abandon may seem an oversimplification, but it helps. Love always trusts. That seems so over the top. But when the currency of trust is consciously valued in the body, much work is accomplished in short order. When trust is lacking or hindered, the work struggles. Diligently keeping and applying the tools of Matthew 18, 1 Corinthians 5, and 1 Timothy 5:17-21 for conflict resolution make a world of difference. Trust rests on transparency and on letting the Word of God truly light our way for maintaining trust.

EZEKIEL 43:5–11—TWO THRESHOLDS

In 1998, I was introduced to Pastor Ray McMillian. A friend and mentor of mine, Pastor Rodney Dukes, was hosting Ray's church at Montgomery AG in Cincinnati while building their own facility. None of us yet had a very developed theology of church-like-heaven-on-earth. But we sensed a growing and earnest compulsion to work more intentionally across racial lines in the church. Rodney and Ray were modeling that.

In late 1998, we invited Ray and Rodney to join us when a few cross-racial pairings of pastors met monthly to begin working on the deepest church divide in our city, the black/white fracture. We started by exploring commonly held racial myths that are painful and divisive. We talked honestly.

At an early meeting, Ray challenged us to go deeper. What he introduced nearly destroyed the group. Ray wanted to know why so many white pastors and Christians venerate the Founding Fathers of America as spiritual heroes in the church and for the church? Why do we pine for some supposed earlier era of greater Christianity in America? Ray was getting at the nationalism in the church, the white part of the church. But he was an equal opportunity offender and didn't let the African American pastors off the hook as to how they might venerate Malcolm X and Martin Luther King Jr., also men not noted for an on-fire personal walk with Jesus.

Some of us were incensed, me included. This was not what we were working on. We were working on reconciliation, relationships, going deeper, not on increasing division through things irrelevant, or so I thought. I really didn't believe this was a problem in the American church; and if it was, it was dying off with the older leaders. Wow was I wrong, as unfolding decades have proven!

I won't share much more on that story as I've also referenced it earlier (chapter 43). But I wanted to share that snippet to set up the hindrance of Two Thresholds.

Ezekiel 43 presents an amazing aspect of the prophet's new temple vision—the temple not yet built, the temple design that metaphorically foreshadows the body of Jesus, the new covenant temple of the Holy Spirit (Ephesians 2:21-22), as I described in Part VI.

Let's read it:

> Then the Spirit lifted me up and brought me into the inner court, and the glory of the LORD filled the temple. While the man was standing beside me, I heard someone speaking to me from inside the temple. He said: "Son of man, this is the place of my throne and the place for the soles of my feet. This is where I will live among the Israelites forever. The people of Israel will never again defile my holy name—neither they nor their kings—by their prostitution and the funeral *offerings for their kings at their death*. When they placed their threshold next to my threshold and their doorposts beside my doorposts, *with only a wall between me and them*, they defiled my holy name by their detestable practices. So I destroyed them in my anger. Now let them put away from me their *prostitution and the funeral offerings for their kings*, and I will live among them forever.
>
> "Son of man, describe the temple to the people of Israel, that they may be ashamed of their sins. Let them consider its perfection, and if they are ashamed of all they have done, make known to them the design of the temple—its arrangement, its exits and entrances—its whole design and all its regulations and laws. Write these down before them so that they may be faithful to its design and follow all its regulations." (Ezekiel 43:5-11, emphasis mine)

The people of God had been guilty of making offerings to dead kings *in the temple!*

The first time Pastor Ray shared this in a 2005 Dallas meeting of national pastors, we were speechless. It was a revelational moment. Someone sitting near Dr. Tony Evans heard him whisper, "Whoa." Yeah. We were all dumbfounded.

Why?

Because here Scripture so clearly declares to the people of God not to mess around with any form of ancestor or hero worship. Yet this is what we as white evangelicals were effectively doing whenever we elevated the founders of America as heroes in the church or elevating black evangelicals (such as King or Malcolm X) as heroes in the church.

Sure America can do so, and we live here. But to bring that into the church alongside His "threshold" where we worship our King of kings, "with only a wall separating," offends the living God—not to mention separating brothers and sisters in Jesus from one another when those "heroes" perpetrated or propped up evil against some of our ancestors.

We pastors in the meeting that day were never going to be the same about this issue.

Through Pastor McMillian, the Lord was revealing a key wedge and powerful hindrance to the vision and the reality of the church Jesus paid for. Millennia before, the Holy Spirit through Ezekiel spoke this for the future people of God. Then Paul wrote:

> For through him we both [nations and Jews] have access to the Father by one Spirit. Consequently, you are no longer foreigners and strangers, but fellow citizens with God's people and also members of his household, built on the foundation of the apostles and prophets, with Christ Jesus himself as the chief cornerstone. In him the whole building is joined together and rises to become a holy temple in the Lord. And in him you too are being built together to become a dwelling in which God lives by his Spirit. (Ephesians 2:18-22)

So whatever it takes, destroy the adulterous threshold. The Lord won't abide two thresholds, one for Him and one for dead kings. Over the unadulterated temple is the place of His throne, and from there He places the soles of His feet, exercises His domain (Ezekiel 43:6-7). "He said: 'Son of man, this is the place of my throne and the place for the soles of my feet. This is where I will live among the Israelites forever. The people of Israel will never again defile my holy name—neither they nor their kings—by their prostitution and the funeral offerings for their kings at their death" (Ezekiel 43:7).

PART VIII

Solutions and Tools

LOVE

Fear will win the day if you don't root your heart in love—rooted in love for people, all people, even those who oppose you, and rooted in love for the plan of God (Acts 20:27). In 1 John 4, writing from the city of Ephesus, "the disciple Jesus loved" writes: "There is no fear in love. But perfect love drives out fear.... Whoever claims to love God yet hates a brother or sister is a liar. For whoever does not love their brother and sister, whom they have seen, cannot love God, whom they have not seen" (1 John 4:18, 20). But here's what I want to emphasize: "there is *no fear* in love." No fear of loss, fear of the other, fear of change and discomfort, fear that you're doing it wrong, fear of . . . you name it—mature love casts that out.

WISDOM

Many new challenges will come your way as you lead into this vision. Hence, your regular cry to God for wisdom is your friend. "If any of you lacks wisdom [knowing what to do, or what is the discerning thing to do], you should ask God, who gives generously to all without finding fault [thinking you're stupid or weak], and it will be given to you" (James 1:5). This can't be overstated. Ask God for wisdom every time you are in a conundrum, which will be often. Why? Because this is difficult. But it's also what Jesus paid for with His blood, and He will have what He paid for.

LISTENING

"Everyone should be quick to listen, slow to speak and slow to become angry" (James 1:19). This is my personal weakness. I am so fast to speak, often before people finish even a sentence. But reconciling ministry requires the opposite. Not that we aren't also vulnerable and sharing equally, but individually, we don't have all the answers. In diversely united church, we are constantly learning, stretching, growing, and receiving as well as giving. Listening fast and speaking slow defeats more challenges than can be counted. I'm still learning this one.

READING

As spoken to in the Praxis section of this book, educate yourself in history, nations, movements, and biographies. Use films, music, articles, books, and Wikipedia. Do whatever you can to get from care to empathy. This will quickly move you into being a more effective reconciler.

IN CHRIST, ALREADY DEAD

"I have been crucified with Christ" (Galatians 2:20). I no longer live, not for myself or my people alone but for Christ and all that He is about. He is about preparing a bride of every tribe, nation, and people. Preferences, ease, comfort, and efficiency are all natural but are not what I live for. I'm dead. This is a great tool for helping the whole church overcome reconciliation-busting challenges.

FASTING AND PRAYER

We have different weapons than this world. Not through our will or strength of will, although these are important, not through manipulation or argumentation, and not by worldly power of any kind will this vision be walked out "but by my Spirit says the Lord" (Zechariah 4:6). And our spirit strengthened through denying our flesh through fasting and applying our hearts to earnest and fervent prayer. So much could be said here, but many others who can do so better than I. So I simply say, "Pray in the Spirit on all occasions with all kinds of prayers and requests. With this in mind, be alert and always keep on praying for *all the Lord's people*" (Ephesians 6:18, italics mine).

TRUTH-TELLING-IN-LOVE KIND OF UNITY

Unity that is surface is no unity at all. Unity seated in truth and love is palpable, powerful, and persuasive. "By this [all people] will know that you are my disciples, if you love one another" (John 13:35). Unity that is among diverse people, rooted in the love and truth of Christ, provides a captivating apologetic for the veracity of the gospel. To get that kind of unity requires honesty in humility, respect, and reciprocity, and leads to authentic, magnetic unity.

FERVOR

So many roadblocks and chasms in your path will come against walking out this vision that a fire in your gut is required. "Never be lacking in zeal, but keep your spiritual fervor, serving the Lord" (Romans 12:11). Paul wrote this to the diverse church at Rome right after having just taught "each member belongs to all the others" and "be devoted to one another in love" (Romans 12:5, 10). Without fervor, we will grow weary! With weariness, the work stalls. Fuel the fire!

FOCUS

Ordinary and extraordinary distractions will fray the focus day in and day out as we apply ourselves to building the Kingdom as the church-like-heaven-on-earth. Quiet in the soul is required. Focus is a fruit of the quiet soul. Be self-aware. Be accountable to others. Have regular checkpoints and evaluations of how you're doing, and of *what* you are doing. Keep your focus. "Keep watch over yourselves and *all the flock* . . . which *he bought with his own blood*. . . . So be on your guard! Remember for three years I never stopped warning each of you night and day with tears" (Acts 20:28, 31, italics mine), exclaimed Paul to the Ephesian elders in his last church meeting before his final arrest to the Ephesian elders, the leaders of the church at Ephesus—the model one new humanity church, the mystery-of-Christ church, the blood-bought, diversely united body of believers Jesus paid for on the Cross. He said this to them.

PRAYER

Pray that we might "fearlessly make known *the mystery of the gospel*" (Ephesians 6:19, in light of Ephesians 3:4-6).

EPILOGUE

Many, many times through the years I've been asked, "How did this all start in your life?"

Fair question. My simple and true answer—the Lord.

As I said, this is true ... and it obviously doesn't satisfy.

So let me tell the story of what actually happened, *what* He actually did. I will trace three threads.

THE FIRST THREAD:
BRIAN WELLS AND CROSSROADS

Brian and Nancy were serving as volunteer leaders of young adult ministries at our church in the early 1990s. It was a crisp, cool November morning in 1994 and I was scheduled for lunch with Brian.

As the Adult Ministries pastor, I was thankful and excited about the growth of this ministry "under" my purview. The group of twentysomethings that was meeting in the Wells home was growing and might soon need to multiply to a couple of more homes. This was the conversation percolating in my heart that morning as I prepared my thoughts to connect with Brian over lunch. Going into 1995, we should identify some new leaders and homes to multiply the group.

After some small talk and catching up with each other, Brian broached the subject that had stirred him to set our meeting. "Chris, Nancy and I are praying about planting a new church with some of our friends. We're in a couples' small group with people from three other churches. We all met at a Christian singles ministry in town, married, and have continued our friendships in the Lord while plugged into different churches."

I remember feeling the blood draining from my face as he talked.

He went on. "We have so many friends we want to invite to church and into a relationship with Christ, but they would never try one of our churches. We have it in our hearts to plant a church together to reach our friends. A different expression of church, one whose services and culture are designed with them in mind." Brian's voice and humility were earnest, sincere. I knew this man's character and walk with Christ, and I trusted that he had prayed on this, thought on it, and was now taking deliberate steps of obedience to the Lord.

For several years since seminary, I had been thinking and praying about the importance of planting new churches to reach people in our society who were far from Jesus. During my last year at Regent University, I studied C. Peter Wagner's *Church Planting for a Greater Harvest* and the current best practices in church multiplication at the time.

On our arrival in Cincinnati joining staff at our current church, Jan and I had discovered an intense reticence for starting new churches—not only within the leadership in our local assembly but also in the church of Cincinnati at large, and in my own network, the Assemblies of God. This had frustrated me to no end. How were we to grow the Kingdom in our city if we didn't plant new churches? Territorialism, fear of cost, fear of failure, and jealousies ruled the day in the church climate of our city. In several clergy meetings in the early 1990s, I wondered out loud, "How do we expect to see lost people won to Jesus and our city changed when we don't apply missions principles at home—the very principles yielding so much fruit overseas?" Older pastors were palpably agitated by my youthful naïveté, as I think they saw me (justifiably so), and yet also at the truth in the questions.

Now over lunch in November 1995, one of the sharpest leaders I've ever worked with, who had encouraged my life and early ministry profoundly, who had joined me in the first leader development cohort I ever led, was asking me for my blessing to leave with some of our young adults and start a new church!

Everything within me felt like my right shoulder and arm were about to be separated from my body. I wanted to say, "Wait, Brian. Things are multiplying, growing so well under your leadership." But the words I heard come out of my mouth sounded more like a question: "How can I help?" That was the Lord. I'm still consciously thankful for the Spirit's help that day in that moment. Had He not helped me, would discouraging words from my selfishness, fear, and doubts have hindered the birthing of what later became Crossroads Church? Possibly.

"Yes" almost always grows the Kingdom better than "no."

Still learning that one.

By early 1995, the originating Crossroads core team had asked Jan and me to lead the work. We felt a heart tug to former Yugoslavia so strongly, where we had served for a year right out of our undergrad in 1989–90, that we gently declined, so certain our time in Cincinnati was winding down. The team asked if we would walk alongside them until they had a lead pastor. We agreed.

We shared all we had. Encouragement, prayer, insights, what little they were—and our church helped send them to Willow Creek for one of the early Leadership Summits. Our senior pastor at the time, Clyde Miller, was breaking the mold on affirming and adding energy to a new church startup, at cost to himself (he hated "losing" people, like a good shepherd) and his congregation.

One early summer day that year, I was pouring my heart out attempting to recruit a potential lead pastor to the work (initially called The Hyde Park Church Plant Project), a mutual friend that the core group and I had agreed to pursue. His seminary days were winding down and his undergrad had been in Cincinnati, so we hoped that we could woo him back to the city.

As I passionately shared about all God was doing in the city and how catalytic I felt this church plant could be to the Kingdom, Brad kindly suggested that maybe I was feeling the call myself. He pulled a book out of his shoulder bag and slid it across the restaurant table to me saying, "You should check this out. The way you're talking sounds a lot like this leader I heard recently speak on city reaching through united local church efforts." The book was *Primary Purpose: Making It Hard for People to Go to Hell from Your City* by Ted Haggard. In those years, Ted's ministry was blazing a whole new kind of gospel-centered trail for others to follow.

The premise of the book was all of the local churches of a city working collaboratively from a heart of mutual blessing, together raising the water level of the Holy Spirit in a city over time.

Already that spring, any time I drove the primary corridors of Cincinnati, I-71 and I-75, I found myself in the car praying over the city, worshiping the Lord, inviting His presence to saturate the neighborhoods, having visions of increasing belief, deep change, abundant life, flourishing within and out from Cincinnati. So when I read Ted's book, *all* of it resonated.

Before the end of the summer, God would use him to help us. Meanwhile Brad passed on the church plant.

THE SECOND THREAD: MICHAEL DANTLEY, STEVE SJOGREN, AND MARK MILLER

One March morning in 1995, I awoke to a clear heaven-signal on my heart, "Go forge friendship with Steve Sjogren and Michael Dantley."

Steve had planted and was leading the largest Vineyard church in the world at that time. He had also authored, *Conspiracy of Kindness*, which was indeed provoking church culture shift and a new kind of church outreach movement.

Michael was leading Cincinnati's most Kingdom-progressive, gospel-focused and Spirit-embracing, African American congregation. A mega-church for that day as well.

I remember asking the Lord, "Why would these men even receive a calendar appointment from me, an assistant pastor at a midsize church?" How would I even get my foot in the door to get on their schedule, much less "forge a friendship"?

I ignored the directive.

But I didn't forget it.

After reading *Primary Purpose* later that summer, I remembered the March word from the Lord, "Forge friendship with Dantley and with Sjogren." I understood He wanted cross-racial and cross-denominational friendships among pastors to begin the process of uniting His church in the city. Some of that had existed in the church of Cincinnati back in the 1970s but had for the most part come undone, largely due to cross-racial injuries and disappointments. (See chapter 41.)

I also realized my side of the family would be vacationing in Colorado that August near Colorado Springs where New Life Church is, the church

Ted was then pastoring. What struck my heart was that I might have a chance to visit a service there and see if what I was reading was authentically happening there. And if it was, then wow. It could happen in Cincinnati. That was how I felt.

Another thing was taking place. More and more, Jan and I were realizing we were beginning to feel a missionary-like call to Cincinnati like the kind we carried on our hearts for the former Yugoslavia. Just before our drive out West for my grandmother's eightieth birthday and our family reunion/vacation, we attended a public informational meeting about the Hyde Park Church Plant Project to support the team. The energy and attendance at the meeting blew us away. Over a hundred people came together to dream what could be.

The team that week asked us once more to pray about leading the effort pastorally. This time we complied. We would pray. Perhaps what the Lord wanted, we thought, was from a new church startup, an explosive one, from which to generate a uniting church and Kingdom movement in Cincinnati. After all, the core team members were coming with blessing from four or five different churches/denominations already. This was fresh, this was Kingdom. Clearly, God was in it. Maybe we had missed Him earlier in the year when we declined.

Driving out West included one more key component in this story. We stopped in St. Louis to attend our first national meeting of our network, the Assemblies of God. What a cornerstone stop it was. At this meeting, the AG General Council of ministers and churches formally repented for the role of racism in our founding and formation—we had broken fellowship with the leadership of the Church of God in Christ (which is predominantly African American today) and had come out from under African American leadership—Charles H. Mason's, to organize the Assemblies of God. Jan and I wept, and our hearts leaped as our leaders repented and as the current presiding bishop of COGIC provided an expression of forgiveness and delivered the sermon to the entire AG constituency gathered. Historic. Reconciling. Vision-stirring.

God was deeply loading up our hearts with a burden and desire to become racial reconcilers through Jesus Christ in us.

On we drove to Colorado to join up with our family, hearts full. During the weekend in the mountains, I felt a tug on my heart to drive into the

Springs and attend church at New Life that Sunday. My siblings and parents joined Jan and me.

What happened that day helped set the course for the next decades of our lives as Kingdom builders, as diversely united church mobilizers, through the reconciling gospel of Jesus.

Never before had I worshiped in a service with two thousand people, witnessed ten babies dedicated in one setting, worshiped with flags of the nations hanging from the rafters as we worshiped, or heard a sermon titled, "The Kingdom of God," literally. I was astounded. The kind of content I had read in Ted's book was being wholeheartedly, demonstrably lived out in front of our eyes! This church, this leader, and his vision for the whole church to love the whole city and impact all the earth—it was real! To say I was inspired is understating the reality of it. My spirit was on fire, my inner man was exploding with energy and joy.

Before the service that morning, I noticed Ted was present and relaxed, hanging out with the early arrivers in the auditorium, fielding questions, and shepherding his flock. Then during the message, he asked for prayer for an afternoon meeting where he and seven other pastors of different Colorado Springs congregation of various tribes would be meeting to discuss matters of the Kingdom for their city.

Remember, we're answering the question, how did the vision of what we do and are as Peoples Church and Network get started and nourished in my heart?

When the service ended, I was undone. I quietly sat observing people fellowshipping and exiting when I noticed an Arab man, culturally dressed, approach and engage in conversation with Pastor Ted. Even witnessing that moment was striking to me: *The nations are here to be reached!* I thought. Attracted, drawn-in, engaged, fully contributing from their wealth of talent, perspectives, wisdom, experience, and resources.

Sitting next to Jan and me that morning was my brother-in-law, Mark Miller, who suddenly tugged on my sleeve and with urgency in his spirit whispered to me, "Let's go meet him." I knew he meant Ted Haggard.

"No, I'm good," I managed to mumble. Mark didn't relent, and before ten more seconds passed, we were striding down the aisle to meet Pastor Ted.

Like Andrew of the Gospels, Mark Miller has a knack, maybe even a spiritual gift, of perceiving incisive moments and acting to introduce or connect leaders and opportunities. He seems to sense when God is at work in two different people, and he creates a bridging moments.

Having "Andrews" in your life and team to add insight and strength to the mix of "God things" happening in ministry and Kingdom building is a vital advantage to the work. God has used Mark this way on our team for many years in many stunning ways.

This one was a noteworthy moment, as will be evident as this story unfolds.

When we reached the front altar area, Ted was still locked in conversation with the Middle Eastern gentleman. We took a seat on the front row a few meters away.

When Ted finished, Mark jumped to action and caught his attention. As he turned toward us, Ted's eyes locked on mine as we neared each other. Mark, not even introducing himself, sidestepped Ted's outreached hand and introduced him to me as "a pastor from Cincinnati I want you to meet."

With a warm smile, Ted immediately asked, "Do you know Steve Sjogren?"

Now remember just earlier that spring the Lord had prompted me to forge a friendship with Steve (and with Bishop Michael Dantley) and here in mid-August I had still not taken even the first step of obedience. My faith that he would receive me was so low. (Right about now I want to teach on the truth that faith is not a feeling or even an "inkling," though it might start there, but it is usually an action.)

Without even waiting for my response, which was slow to materialize as wheels were turning in my head, Ted pressed his queries, "Is he a Kingdom collaborator in the city?"

Now I was stunned silent again.

The answer was no, but I wasn't going to say it and dishonor my fellow Cincy pastor. So speechless I remained, unsure what to say.

Reading my eyes, Ted deduced, "I didn't think so."

Now I was offended for my home team.

I found my voice. "Why do you say that?"

"Because most megachurch pastors of fast-growing works are drowning. They're drowning in the rapid growth of their church, and they are often totally unaware of the larger Kingdom role they have in a city," he explained.

Now I relaxed.

Wow. Ted provided insight and wisdom for team-building in our city for years to come. He sensed the tension that probably exists in the church in every city—smaller church pastor agitation with the larger church pastors who never seem willing to play team ball, and large church pastors feeling judged and misunderstood. Separated. Divided. Underwhelming our cities with our disunity.

Ted kept talking. "Chris, can you do something for me? Can you get Steve to read *Primary Purpose*? I've invited him to speak at a church leaders' meeting this November in Los Angeles organized by Jack Hayford [an American churchman at that time], Bill Bright [Cru Founder], Loren Cunningham [YWAM Founder], John Dawson [author of *Healing America's Wounds*] and a few others. The whole meeting is about city-reaching through collaboration. Because of Steve Sjogren's fresh ideas on evangelism [*Conspiracy of Kindness* was recently published and having a significant impact on the global church of Jesus Christ], I've invited him to speak. But the thing is, I need him to understand the purpose of the meeting. Can you get him to read *Primary Purpose*?"

"Sure, I'll work on that." And with that the conversation was over.

As we drove back to our vacation spot in the mountains that day, all I could think was this: Now I have a specific, credible reason for reaching out to Steve and thereby begin to obey the Lord's prompting from earlier in the year. God's grace was at work in my life, I reasoned. True, but there was more to it.

My first day back in the office after my August travels shocked my world.

On my desk waiting for me was a letter from Ted Haggard. It was an invitation to the same Los Angeles meeting that coming November I had committed to explain to Steve Sjogren. The invitation was not to me; it was to my senior pastor, Clyde Miller. But in his handwriting across some white space of the cover page of the letter was a note by him to me. "Chris, I want you to go." Clyde knew nothing yet of my interaction with Pastor Ted.

What?!

I briskly walked the hall to Pastor Clyde's office and burst through the door unannounced. "Do you know what this invitation is?" I blurted out, and quickly explained the meeting to him as I understood it from my few moments with Ted Haggard the week before.

Remember, I'm telling this story to help answer this question: "How did God first stir in your heart this vision of church-like-heaven-on-earth?"

He used three threads. This story now is just the middle of the second thread. If these things didn't happen to me personally, I'm not sure I could believe myself all that God did. But He did do all these things, despite my foot-dragging and disbelief many times along the way. The Holy Spirit guided experiences of these days branded into my being the call for what He wanted, and He used them later to anchor my heart when the storms against the vision, and different aspects of the vision, came. And come they did . . . as you've read earlier.

Back to the story. Clyde looked up at me from his desk. Peering over his glasses, he repeated what was in his handwritten note, "Chris, I can't go. I want you to go."

I rejoiced. Not only was I now calling Steve Sjogren to tell him about a conversation I had experienced with Ted Haggard, but I was going to the same meeting!

The letter explained some things, too. The meeting was for pastors from a hundred cities, seven each. The churches chosen were considered to be "anchor churches of the city."

"Who are the other six churches invited from Cincinnati?" I wondered. Going back to my office, I called New Life Church in Colorado Springs to ask how the churches were selected, the seven each from a hundred cities.

Someone called back later with the answer. They chose the one hundred most populated cities in America and then randomly called phone numbers in the city asking this question: "What are the seven most influential churches on the spiritual climate of your city?" Then they invited the pastors of those churches, they explained.

"Can you tell me the other six churches in Cincinnati, please?" I requested. And they told me. One of course was the Cincinnati Vineyard, pastored by Steve Sjogren. Another one was Christ Emmanuel Christian Fellowship, pastored by Bishop Michael Dantley. Oh my.

When I hung up that call, my heart was racing. Not only was there a reason to get on Steve's schedule, there was for Michael's as well. Because of Pastor Clyde's decision to include me on his invitation, I was going to a meeting of national import for the Kingdom of God to which they too were invited. My ask to achieve a spot on their schedule would be, "Can we meet for a few minutes to discuss the purpose of this invite from Ted Haggard and consider attending the meeting together?"

Look at God!

In short, initial meetings took place with both pastors, and deep friendships and collaboration were engendered.

There is a striking amount of Kingdom detail I'm leaving out for the sake of brevity (is that still possible?). Amazing God-stories, but suffice it to say that the Lord went before us in extraordinary ways. He also allowed us to see and experience examples of the intensity of hell's fury that comes against dreams like these: one blood-bought, diversely united church in a city, the whole gospel for all people groups, city after city, nation after nation, in the whole earth, till He comes again.

Interdenominational and racial oneness through His justice and righteousness, because of His gospel, are not easy. But Jesus paid for these things on the cross, and He should have what He paid for. And they are His strategic plan to fulfill His Kingdom come on earth as it is in heaven.

THE THIRD THREAD:
THE WHOLE GOSPEL, FOR THE WHOLE CITY, THROUGH THE WHOLE CHURCH

While we were in Los Angeles that November 1995, some amazing things took place.

Leading up to the trip, the Lord had allowed me to begin my first-ever heart-level friendship with an African American brother, Galen Jones. Galen had served as a deacon where Bishop Michael Dantley was pastoring, and now he was an associate pastor for Pastor Ray McMillian. Michael was one of the two pastors the Lord had spoken to me about in March earlier that year. Later, God was to use Pastor Ray to help me to a "second conversion" if you will, rooting out the "Christian nationalism" in my heart that fed racial superiority and racist tendencies I wasn't even conscious of.

About a hundred pastors from across the country attended the meeting called by Haggard, Heyford, Bright, Dawson, and Cunningham. Five of us were from Cincinnati, the largest single contingency from the hundred cities invited. Galen and I roomed together. That was the beginning of some of the most important friendship-level talks on race and racial history, culture, and the gospel I had ever experienced.

Two other key experiences marked the week.

First, during a discussion led by John Dawson on the power and need for racial reconciliation in the church for there to be healing in society for generations of racialized sin and injustice, one white pastor asked a telling question: "How long will we need to ask for forgiveness?" Dawson's measured and gentle response rocked my world: "Until the hurting stops." Mic drop.

The second was this: That same evening after a day full of Kingdom-thinking sessions and a delightful Italian dinner in downtown LA, four of us sat talking in Steve Sjogrens's rental car outside of Galen's and my hotel. Reflecting on the day, Steve began to weep. As he did so, he began to pray. Soon, from the depths of his soul he was crying out to God to forgive him for his arrogance to believe he could reach a city by himself. Heaving and sobbing, he repented.

All I could think was, "Look at God!" Soon all four of us were praying for Cincinnati together. Black and white, multidenominational, lead and staff pastors, parachurch (Galen worked for City Gospel Mission in our city for his day job) and church, lay leader (Jim Cochran in the back seat, Cincinnati Vineyard's business administrator and a marketplace guy), and clergy. We were missing other equal parts of Kingdom leadership from back home (women and internationals or other ethnic groups) but here we were, two thousand miles from home praying as *one* over our city. I would never be the same.

After we came back from Los Angeles, Galen and I were invited on the citywide Christian radio station to share what we experienced together and what it might mean for Kingdom things in our city. Galen especially began to cast one of the clearest, most compelling Kingdom visions of a racially reconciling, denominationally united, mutual-blessing movement of abundant life for all in our city I had ever heard. We were on fire by His Spirit. And His fire in us burns hot today, twenty-five years later.

There are many new players, and leaders have come and gone, but what Jesus ignited in us that spring, summer, and fall of 1995, in terms of a vision for church-like-heaven-on-earth—the whole church, with the whole gospel, for the whole city—burns red hot. To His glory, alone.

So for me personally and for our church over the next years, God would use many influences and relationships—books, music, films, race history museums, as well as people: Dr. John M. Perkins, Michael O. Emerson, Rose Sherman, Ray McMillian, T. D. Jakes, Tony Evans, Mark DeYmaz, Derwin Gray, Beth Moore, Priscilla Shirer, and many local friends—to grow in me and us as a local church what He had planted in 1995. We were to become a racially reconciling, generationally rich, and thriving local church creating access for all people to Jesus and His Kingdom, loving, living, and proclaiming His full gospel.

Revelation 5:9-10 speaks of the blood purchase of the Lamb: "And they sang a new song, saying: 'You are worthy to take the scroll and open its seals, because you were slain, and with your blood you purchased for God persons from every tribe and language and people and nation. You have made them to be a kingdom and priests to serve our God and they will reign on the earth.'"

And Revelation 10:11, "Then I was told, 'You must prophesy again about many peoples, nations, languages and kings.'"

Followers of Jesus and leaders of His blood purchase, His bride share the vision again and again and again until the trumpet blows.

"The seventh angel sounded his trumpet, and there were loud voices in heaven, which said: 'The kingdom of the world has become the kingdom of our Lord and of his Messiah, and he will reign for ever and ever'" (Revelation 11:15).

ADDENDUMS

DIAGNOSTIC QUESTIONS

1. How do the demographics of the church I serve compare with the demographics of my county/community/city? Think economically, ethnically, politically, generationally, educationally, etc.
2. In what ways does our church leadership reflect the demographics of our community?
3. In what ways might my social media inadvertently offend or scare off any part of my community with cultural or partisan preferences? Might any of my postings make people feel they have to agree with me on nonessential topics before they can attend and experience the gospel?
4. How am I crying out to God for a harvest among all people within our ten-mile reach?
5. What do I know about the different people groups of my city/county/community?
6. In what ways might I study the social challenges and spiritual history of my context, and how we might address those from a Kingdom view?

GLOSSARY OF TERMS

Apostolic—describes a leader who births and builds, is entrepreneurial and visionary, and can raise up leaders and ministries.

Biblical justice—making wrongs right through God's heart of compassion and wise actions, led by His Spirit and the principles of His Word/Kingdom. The Bible-rooted idea of defending the cause of the vulnerable: the fatherless/orphaned; the widowed/elderly; people living with disabilities; the immigrant; the oppressed (see Psalm 82:3; Job 29:10-20). Especially held in contrast to the often-despised idea (by evangelicals) of "social justice." It's a little tougher for us to argue against the straight-up biblical ideas of justice; hence, "biblical justice."

Biznistry—a business that is also a ministry platform and/or is generating revenue for Kingdom building.

Church-like-heaven-on-earth—multi-ethnic, multiracial, multi-economic, multinational, multi-generational church, like what Jesus paid for on the Cross.

Church multiplication—the planting of new churches, especially reproducing churches.

Comfortable with the uncomfortable—embracing sacrifice for the greater good; being willing and able to experience the dissonance that comes with challenging closely held beliefs (excepting Christ and the Cross), personal or cultural values, and preferences through experience, diverse relationships, and greater clarity from Scripture.

Depoliticize—to bleed partisan politics out of something: out of the pulpit, out of personal witness, out of the church. Not to disengage from the political arena, but therein to be equal-opportunity agitators for all political parties. To let our first identity be as ambassadors of another government—the Kingdom of God. To be a political independent who is gospel-centered.

Diverse unity—unity with diversity. Deeper than multi-ethnic. Reconciled. United. One new humanity (see Ephesians 2:14-16).

Equality—sameness in value, respect, and opportunity.

Equity—equal advantage.

Flourishing—healthy, well-supplied, bearing fruit, generous.

Habesha—an Ethiopian (Amharic) word for "people," which is used to collectively describe the Eritrean and Ethiopian people/ethnic/language groups, of which there are more than eighty.

Hive off—an expression in church planting for when a "mother" church seeds a new church plant with people from the parent congregation.

Idolatry of a nation—when love of country outpaces love for our King and His people or the lost.

Inclusion vs. assimilation—respectful, diverse belonging and shared ownership as individuals within an organization, acceptance and participation as equals as opposed to loss of uniqueness in order to belong by conforming culturally, in perspective, or in outlook.

Missions—working cross-culturally to plant the gospel, especially among least reached peoples or toward that end.

Multicultural—intentional inclusion and celebration of diverse cultures as equal within an organization.

Multi-economic—intentional inclusion of diverse class and socioeconomic groups as equals within an organization.

Multi-ethnic—intentional naming, celebrating, and inclusion of diverse ethnic identities and heritages within an organization.

Nationalism—passion for one's own ethnic group or nation at the expense of others.

One new humanity—Paul's expression about the congregation at Ephesus, the diversely reconciled and united people of God as one body through Christ and His Cross (see Ephesians 2:14-16).

Patriotism—affection for one's own country, sometimes superseding one's affection for the Lord or the Kingdom of God, sometimes insensitively or offensively intermingled with Christianity and worship.

Race—a human social construct used to differentiate people of varied ethnic heritage or skin color. However, in America, it also is the *lingua franca* (the language of the land) for discussing matters relevant to African Americans and matters affected by black and white relations, historical and present. To avoid the word "race" or the related subjects, or to subsume it into the idea that *there's only one human race*, which is of course, true, but can be unwittingly, and unintentionally perhaps, used to avoid the difficult topic of black/white relations and racial history in America.

Racial justice—things morally wrong and unfair toward African Americans historically and now, the prior and current repercussions, and the remaining and persistent resulting deficits, made right.

Racial reconciliation—when loving relationship and biblical/racial justice meet.

Racialization—when matters are influenced by black and white irreconciliation or injustice.

Racism—the sin of "dismissive othering," disdain, hatred, prejudice, bias and/or fear, unconscious and/or conscious, and the intended and/or unintended consequences therefrom.

Redlining—intentional rules and banking practices prohibiting loans to people of color.

Societal righteousness—another way to think about biblical justice.

USAGWM—the United States Assemblies of God world missions team. Soon we will see the Kenyan Assemblies of God World Missions (KAGWM), Tanzanian Assemblies of God World Missions (TAGWM), Brazilian Assemblies of God World Missions (BAGWM)—hence, the need to differentiate our language and not simply use AGWM, or Assemblies of God World Missions, for the US expression. There's a humility in this, as well as a practical wisdom.

UPGs—Unreached People Groups, distinct socioethnic, linguistic groups without reproducing gospel-centered churches and/or less than 2 percent gospel-centered Christianity. (See JoshuaProject.net.)

RESOURCE LIST

ARTICLES/EXPERIENCES

"Church Like Heaven on Earth," Christopher N. Beard, *Influence*, March/April 2016

"Diversity, Donations, and Disadvantage," Samuel Perry (what we need to know about support raising for ethnic minorities, especially African American missionaries)

"Ephesian Model," Christopher N. Beard, *Influence*, July/Aug 2018

Ephesus, the archeological site, western Turkey (life-altering to me)

FOCUS, a strategic planning experience/game for ministry leadership teams (ElementalChurches.com)

"How A Once-White Church Broke Down Racial Barriers," NPR, August 30, 2015 (Peoples Church Cincinnati on NPR)

"How Churches Are Slowly Becoming Less Segregated," *Wall Street Journal*, October 13, 2014 (covering the multi-ethnic church movement in the United States, and a case study look into Peoples Church Cincinnati)

Jackson Hole, Wyoming (where I wrote some of this book)

Multiethnic Conversations, DeYmaz and Okuwobi (a twelve-week daily devotional and weekly small group curriculum)

"Obama could have a prayer among Ohio's white evangelicals," *LA Times*, May 19, 2012 (a front-page story that included Peoples Church Cincinnati)

"The Case for Reparations," Ta-Nehisi Coates, *The Atlantic* (which God used to stir my heart profoundly about the biblical idea of restitution for people of African descent in the United States)

Undivided, Chuck Mingo and Lynn Watts (a six-week small group experience)

BOOKS

(In prioritized order of impact on my life and leadership since 1995)

The One Year Bible

Let Justice Roll Down, John M. Perkins

Divided by Faith, Michael O. Emerson and Christian Smith

United by Faith, DeYoung, Emerson, Yancey, and Kim

Letters Across the Divide, David Anderson

The Search for Christian America, Noll, Marsden, and Hatch

Multicultural Ministry Handbook, David Anderson and Margarita Cabellon

Why the Bell Can't Ring: Legacy of a Divided House, Ray McMillian

W. E. B. DuBois, biography in two volumes, David Levering Lewis

Souls of Black Folk, W. E. B. DuBois

The LiveDead Journal, Dick Brogden

The Weary Blues, Langston Hughes

With Christ in the School of Prayer, Andrew Murray

I Know Why the Caged Bird Sings, Maya Angelou

The New Jim Crow, Michelle Alexander

Gracism: The Art of Inclusion, David A. Anderson

Generous Justice, Timothy Keller

Just Mercy, Brian Stevenson

Many Colors, Soong-Chan Rah

The Root of the Righteous, A. W. Tozer

The Post-Black and Post-White Church, Efrem Smith

Mere Christianity, C. S. Lewis

The Seven Storey Mountain, Thomas Merton

The Color of Law, Richard Rothstein

Hero Maker, Dave Ferguson and Warren Bird

Bridging the Diversity Gap, Alvin Sanders

E. M. Bounds on Prayer

Empowering Leadership, Michael Fletcher

Ready, Set, Grow, Scott Wilson

The Return of the Prodigal Son, Henri Nouwen

The Color of Compromise, Jemar Tisby

Live Dead Joy, Dick Brogden

FerVent, Priscilla Shirer

Between the World and Me, Ta-Nehisi Coates

The Next Evangelicalism, Soong-Chan Rah

Myth of a Christian Nation, Gregory Boyd

Medical Apartheid, Harriet A. Washington

Christian Origins in Ephesus and Asia Minor, Mark Fairchild

Mystery, Mark S. Kinzer

Embrace, Leroy Barber

Surprised by Hope, N. T. Wright

One Blood, John M. Perkins

Building a Healthy Multi-ethnic Church, Mark DeYmaz

Leading a Healthy Multi-ethnic Church, Mark DeYmaz

The Coming Revolution in Church Economics, Mark DeYmaz

Five Years to Life, Sam Huddleston

Commissioned to Love, John P. Perkins

NOVELS

Dominion, by Randy Alcorn

Heaven, by Randy Alcorn

Roots, by Alexander Haley

MOVIES

13th

Amistad

Antwoine Fisher

Barbershop

Black Panther

BlacKkKlansman

Boyz n the Hood

Do the Right Thing

Glory

Jazz (documentary by Ken Burns)

Just Mercy

Malcolm X

Remember the Titans

Roots

Selma

Slavery by Another Name, NPR

The Butler

The Help

Tuskegee Airmen

Twelve Years a Slave

MUSEUMS AND MEMORIALS

Martin Luther King, Jr. Memorial—Washington, DC (nps.gov/mlkm)

National Museum of African American History & Culture—Washington DC (nmaahc.si.edu)

National Underground Railroad Freedom Center—Cincinnati, OH (freedomcenter.org)

The Legacy Museum—Montgomery, AL (museumandmemorial.eji.org)

The National Memorial for Peace & Justice—Montgomery, AL (museumandmemorial.eji.org)

MUSIC

Armstrong, Louis

Boyz II Men

Charles, Ray

DC Talk, *Jesus Freak* project

Franklin, Kirk

Hammond, Fred

Hawthorne, Koryn

Holiday, Billie

Lecrae

Marsalis, Wynton

McClurkin, Donnie
Parker, Charlie
Tedashii
Today's Gospel Hits
Tribbett, Tye
Walls Group
Yolanda

PEOPLES CHURCH NETWORK OFFERINGS

ACCESS, small group curriculum (peopleschurch.co)

ACCESS Booklet, above-tithe giving to grow the Kingdom (peopleschurch.co)

Committed, small group curriculum (peopleschurch.co)

Crossonomics, small group curriculum

Finally Making Money, Dorothy & Brandon Wilkes (Amazon.com)

Inclusion, Reggie Lenzy (our four-step on-ramping experience for new attenders)

Journey: Road Map to Your Faith, Derek Sanborn (Amazon.com)

Justice Team Guidelines (peopleschurch.co)

Language Ministry Guidelines (peopleschurch.co)

Leadership Pathway (peopleschurch.co)

Missions Guidelines (peopleschurch.co)

The Vision Experience, small group curriculum

DENOMINATIONAL RESOLUTIONS

Assemblies of God Resolutions on Race 1989, 1995, 2015
Presbyterian Church of America Resolution on Race 2016
Southern Baptist Convention Resolution on Race 1995

VIDEOS

"Churches Hold 'Black Lives Matter' Sunday," CNN Morning Show, December 2014

"How to Fix Racism in America," T. D. Jakes

"Race, Culture and Christ," Tony Evans

WEBSITES

CarePortal.org

CoalitionOfCare.org (mobilizing the church for vulnerable children)

EJI.org (Brian Stevenson)

ElementalChurches.com (Dave Workman)

JoshuaProject.net

LiveDead.org

Mosaix.Info

OhioJPC.org

PeoplesChurch.co

TheWitnessFoundation.co (Jemar Tisby's foundation for funding black Christian ministries to the glory of God)

Voices-Project.org (influencing culture through training and promoting leaders of color)